FOUNDATIONS
of
CHRISTIAN MYSTICISM

Scharl van Staden TRM

Artwork done by Throne Room Mystic

All images generated using AI - ChatGPT image creator

Typesetting/layout - Seraph Creative

First Edition: May 2025

ISBN: 978-1-964959-50-4

eBook: 978-1-964959-51-1

Published by Seraph Creative in 2025

United States / United Kingdom / South Africa / Australia

www.seraphcreative.org

Bible references used from The NIV Translation, The Amplified Version and The Passion Translation.

Foundations of Christian Mysticism is the result of personal study, spiritual encounter, and theological reflection by the author. Portions of this book were developed, edited, and refined with the assistance of language tools, to enhance clarity, structure, and stylistic flow.

"The Infinite cannot be grasped except through unknowing." - Bereshit

CONTENTS

*Christ in you, the
hope of glory.*

Introduction

To the modern Christian, mysticism may appear as a mysterious and esoteric concept associated with new age and the occult, filled with symbols, paradoxes, and seemingly weird practices. However, Christian mysticism is not a contaminated belief system but the most intimate reality, the divine essence intertwined with the very fabric of existence. It serves as a current flowing beneath the surface of faith, pulling the soul deeper into the essence of God. The goal of this book is not just to explain Christian mysticism, but to awaken readers to its living essence. It unveils hidden mysteries, leading those who wish to see with their hearts and tune in the Spirit's quiet voice. Christian mysticism is not a creation of medieval monks or a mere adoption of Eastern traditions; it is intricately woven into the foundation of scripture. The prophets witnessed God's glory, Jesus shared the mysteries of the Kingdom, and Paul revealed the greatest mystery as "Christ in you, the hope of glory." The secrets of God are not concealed; they are unveiled to those who seek, to those whose thirst for the divine cannot be quenched by mere words.

THE CALL TO THE MYSTIC PATH

Every generation produces those who are called beyond the surface of faith, those who sense an invitation echoing within their souls, a longing that no earthly fulfilment can satisfy. This longing is the seed of mysticism, the holy desire that leads from mere belief into the depths of divine union. But this journey is not one of striving or intellectual mastery. It is a path of surrender, an invitation to become still enough to hear the whispers of eternity.

Mysticism is often misunderstood. It is not about rejecting reason or having secret knowledge, not for others. Rather, it is a way of life that offers a deeper understanding beyond the ordinary frameworks of traditional Christianity. Mysticism is about harmonising the soul with the rhythms of God's presence and recognising the sacred in all things. It involves delving into a radiant darkness where God reveals Himself not through concepts but through personal encounters and mystical ecstasies and joys. The path of the mystic leads to enlightenment and, ultimately, unity, where the false self is shed to reveal the authentic self, the primordial image concealed in God. This is the transformation of consciousness that Paul describes when he speaks of putting on the mind of Christ. It is the path of the Desert Fathers and Mothers, the ecstatic visions of Hildegard of Bingen, the dark night of John of the Cross, the celestial ascent of Meister Eckhart, and the divine intimacy of Julian of Norwich. Each mystic, in their own way, has walked this path, leaving behind footprints to follow.

THE LANGUAGE OF MYSTICISM: BETWEEN THE SEEN AND THE UNSEEN

Mysticism defies simple definition as it speaks a language of paradox. In this realm, darkness (as in the mystery) outshines light, surrender leads to victory, and the greatest knowledge is found in unknowing. The term "mystic" comes from the Greek word mystikos, which translates to "hidden" or "secret." This concealed nature is not meant to keep us away but to draw us closer. God's mysteries are not hidden to obstruct our view but to deepen our desire to explore. As Jesus told His disciples, "It has been given to you to know the mysteries of the Kingdom." This book explores different aspects of Christian mysticism: the contemplative practices that open the soul to divine experiences, the biblical and historical origins of the mystical journey, the sacred geometry and divine patterns that reveal God's essence in creation, and the ecstatic encounters that have shaped the lives of those who have glimpsed divine reality. Mysticism isn't about escaping the world; it's about deep engagement and its unfolding in creation. Mystics encounter God in every aspect of life.

ENTERING THE SACRED MYSTERY

This book immerses you into an ancient and vibrant culture, inviting you to join a community that has longed for a connection with God beyond words, religion, and tradition. It encourages exploration of divinity not as a distant concept but as a constant presence that unites all of existence. The Christian mystical journey doesn't lead away from Christ but deeper into His essence. He is both the ultimate destination and the very path; the gateway and the one who knocks. Prepare yourself not only for a mental journey, but for a profound transformation of your spirit. Allow this book to illuminate your path and guide you into the luminous mystery where God lives.

> The proclamation of Jesus is "according to the revelation of the mystery that was kept secret for long ages".
> (Romans 16:25)
>
> God's wisdom is described as "secret and hidden."
> (1 Corinthians 2:7)
>
> Followers of Jesus are "stewards of God's mysteries."
> (1 Corinthians 4:1)
>
> The secrets of the kingdom of heaven.
> (Matthew 13:11)
>
> In 1 Corinthians 13 (the famous "love" chapter), Saint Paul

notes that, even if he could "understand all mysteries and all knowledge," if he lacked love, he would be "nothing." Belief in life after death is described as a mystery. (1 Corinthians 15:51)

In Ephesians 1:9, the "mystery of [God's] will" has, according to God's good pleasure, been "set forth in Christ."

In Colossians 1:26–27, the mystery of God is described as hidden throughout the ages, but now revealed; the mystery is "Christ in you, the hope of glory."

In Colossians 2:2, "God's mystery" is described as "Christ himself." In the first letter to Timothy, there are references to the "mystery of the faith" (3:9) and the "mystery of our religion" (3:16), which is explained in terms of events from the life of Jesus.15

Let the same mind be in you that was in Christ Jesus, who, though he was in the form of God, did not regard equality with God as something to be exploited, but emptied himself, taking the form of a slave, being born in human likeness. —Apostle Paul
(Philippians 2:5–7)

"Through these he has given us his very great and precious promises, so that through them you may participate in the divine nature, having escaped the corruption in the world caused by evil desires."
(2 Peter 1:4)

...the path to unlocking union is characterised by discipline, silence, and reframing

Mysticism In Christianity

The role of mysticism in Christianity can be elusive and complex, easily overlooked or misunderstood by institutional churches and their leadership. For centuries, mysticism has remained on the periphery of mainstream Christianity because of an intricate web of historical, theological, and ecclesiastical factors. Many pastors, priests, and other religious leaders often shy away from discussions on mysticism. They struggle to understand its significance in spiritual life because of common misunderstandings and the fear of being misinterpreted. As a result, they find the topic unsettling and unorthodox.

There's no doubt that the word 'mysticism' itself can create a sense of doubt and confusion due to the fact that non-Christian societies and groups have adopted practices and lifestyles under the banner of mysticism and therefore created this veil between what is Christian and what is not, based on association. The suffix -ism carries specific meanings and functions when attached to words like mysticism. It typically shows a system of beliefs, principles, or practices. I clearly remember my Theology professor explicitly warning us against embracing any '-ism' as an extreme ideology. In the case of mysticism, the -ism emphasises the idea of an organised or systematic approach to mystical experiences, such as the belief in direct communication with God or a transcendent reality. I've come to learn that in traditional beliefs, an 'ism' refers to a departure from the conventional and the adoption of a set of beliefs that challenge conformists and those seeking control. Beyond systems of belief, -ism can also describe a characteristic state or condition, as in heroism. It frequently denotes ideologies, movements, or schools of thought, like feminism or capitalism. The suffix itself originates from the Greek -ismos and Latin -ismus, which were used to denote a specific set of actions, conditions, or practices. In mysticism, -ism highlights that the concept extends beyond a formalised practice or doctrine of seeking spiritual insight. Essentially, -ism serves to transform a root word into something outside the norm, branching into a specific concept or system. This makes mysticism more than just a singular experience — it represents an ongoing belief system focused on attaining a deeper connection with higher realities through contemplation or direct experience.

This fuels and reflects a broader sentiment among contemporary Christians that the language and concepts of mysticism, with their focus on mystery, paradox, darkness, and the ineffable can seem strange and intimidating. For many, there is a clear separation between having a direct and personal relationship with Jesus and the deeper, often abstract, divine union that mysticism advocates. This struggle isn't new and has its roots deep in Christian history.

From research by Carl McColman: Around fifteen centuries ago, a writer known under the pseudonym Dionysius the Areopagite noticed that Christian tradition operates with two distinct modes: one that is mystical, shrouded in symbolism and mystery, and another that is more apparent, accessible, and philosophical. Mysticism offers a path to divine union through experiences that transcend explanation or instruction. In contrast, the open tradition relies on logical persuasion and clear, academic, and sermon-like instruction. Thus, throughout Christian history, two parallel paths have emerged. In the first aspect, which is more visible and public, faith is portrayed as a moral system or a collection of rituals that coincide with significant events in life. These events include salvation, baptism, the infilling of the Holy Spirit, marriage, and many more. This path focuses on God's love and the promise of heaven AFTER death. The second, more esoteric path, the mystical way, emphasises inner transformation, seeking not to prepare for heaven when we die but to allow God's presence to permeate your being in the HERE AND NOW, starting a process of discovering the oneness and union we have with Him. In essence, mysticism aims to reveal heaven within us, the here and now, rather than merely getting us into heaven.

Despite its availability to all who love Jesus, this mystical path remains hidden to many Christians. Lack of exposure or insight causes misunderstanding and misinterpretation, leading to the mystical path's ignorance, and criticism. The reasons for this are manifold, some rooted in the historical upheavals of the church, particularly the Protestant Reformation, which altered perceptions of spiritual authority and their practices.

The Protestant Reformation, which began in the 16th century, was a pivotal event that reshaped Western Christianity. Reformers like Martin Luther and John Calvin emphasised scripture alone and a faith accessible to all believers. Prioritising scripture and reason reduced space for mystical experience and subjectivity. Mystics, who often emphasised direct experiences of God that transcended rational understanding, found themselves increasingly marginalised. Because their insights were not always verifiable by scripture or reason, people treated them with suspicion, skepticism, and sometimes branded them as heresy. The Reformation's focus on personal salvation and justification by faith sometimes overshadowed the mystical goal of union with God through contemplative practices. The result was a Christianity that leaned more heavily on preaching, teaching, and communal worship rather than the solitary and inward-focused practices characteristic of mysticism.

Besides the Reformation, the Enlightenment movement further solidified this divide. The extreme of rationalism and the opposite, empiricism, with its reliance on experience alone to knowledge, became dominant modes of thought, influencing theology and spirituality. Mysticism, with its reliance on experiences beyond rational comprehension, appeared out of step with the growing emphasis on scientific reasoning and observable evidence. Churches, eager to remain relevant, focused on ethical living, clear doctrines and social engagement, rather than the more obscure and demanding path of contemplation and the inner sanctuary.

Beyond historical factors, the very nature of mysticism presents challenges to mainstream Christianity. Unlike regular church attendance or participation in sacraments, mysticism demands an ongoing commitment to practices that are often arduous and devoid of immediate gratification. Contemplative prayer, meditation, and interaction with the spirit realm require patience, humility, and a willingness to embrace uncertainty and silence. It is a journey of ascension, unlocking position and the oneness we enjoy in Christ. The modern world, with its emphasis on entertainment, productivity, and sensory stimulation, offers little encouragement for such practices.

Mysticism also disrupts the comfortable equilibrium that many Christians find in established religious routines. Conventional church life often asks for manageable levels of commitment: attending services, taking part in community activities, and living a moral life. In return, believers are assured of God's love and care, both in this life and the next. Mysticism, however, calls for a more radical transformation, a dying self, an emptying of ego, and a relentless pursuit of divine union. You might feel that there are similarities, but mysticism insists that the journey of union with God is not merely about moral living or doctrinal belief but about a complete surrender to the mystery of the divine. Mysticism does not guarantee clear answers or immediate spiritual highs, though in time, they unfold. Throughout my years as a mystic, I have unfortunately observed people reverting to traditional church practices, be it evangelical or denominational, after experiencing the initial journey and transformation of their thoughts and actions as too radical. This shift occurs because they seek more immediate gratification. The mystical journey often involves periods of dryness, where God's presence seems distant or entirely absent. Yet mystics maintain God is always present, working in the depths of the soul, even when the conscious mind senses nothing extraordinary. This 'dry' period involves shifting from the current state of Christianity to its original primordial form. For many, this lack of guaranteed experience is daunting. Contemporary culture, conditioned to expect quick results and tangible outcomes, struggles with the ambiguity inherent in mysticism. While the promise of union with God may seem alluring, the path to unlocking union is characterised by discipline, silence, and reframing. However, this path may appear too arduous for many to undertake.

Despite these challenges, mysticism remains a vital aspect of Christian spirituality. In an age marked by anxiety, distraction, and superficiality, the mystical path offers a counter-narrative. It invites believers to slow down, enter the depths of their own souls, and encounter God in profound new pathways of contemplation. While not everyone feels called or wants to embrace the mystical path, those who do discover a wellspring of spiritual vitality that transcends dogma and ritual.

Mysticism also reminds the church of the mystery at the heart of faith. Christianity is more than just a collection of beliefs or ethical guidelines. Instead, it encompasses a vibrant, living relationship with a transcendent God who exceeds the limits of human understanding. The mystical preserves this sense of wonder, offering a corrective to overly rational or institutional expressions of faith. In doing so, it bridges the gap between the logical and the spiritual realms.

In conclusion, the marginalisation of mysticism within mainstream Christianity is understandable due to historical, theological, and cultural dynamics. However, the mystical path continues to offer a profound invitation to inner transformation and divine union. Although it may not be appealing to everyone, its presence within the broader Christian faith ensures that the church remains open to the full depth and mystery of the divine encounter. Those who are drawn to this path will find a deep heritage of wisdom and practice that leads them not only to belief but to the heart of God in a completely new and deep way.

...cultivating a lifestyle of divine union unlocking the manifestation of Christ in you

Grappling With The Mystery Of Mysticism

"For my thoughts are not your thoughts, nor are your ways my ways, declares the Lord." —Isaiah 55:8

Mysticism, particularly within the Christian realm, dwells in dimensions beyond the reach of human language. Though different aspects of the mystical journey can be recounted and explored, one essential truth remains constant: the essence of mysticism is inherently elusive. This ineffability — the inability of words to fully encapsulate mystical experience — pervades every narrative and every dimension of the mystical path. Therefore, with humility and openness, we need to approach this topic by acknowledging that all descriptions will ultimately fall short. The heart of the mystical experience resists the confines of speech and definition.

THE PARADOX OF DEFINING THE UNDEFINABLE

Attempting to define mysticism is like trying to measure limitlessness, an exercise in futility. Limitless transcends temporal and spatial boundaries. It is a spiritual reality that defies categorisation or quantification. Similarly, mysticism, which embodies a profound encounter with limitless divine love, evades all attempts at confinement within the structures of human language and intellect. Even the most inspired poetic language can only gesture toward its reality. Words, at best, can evoke or hint at the mystical; they cannot encapsulate it. To try to explain mysticism is like attempting to drain the vastness of the sea with a single spoonful.

> "Can you fathom the mysteries of God?
> Can you probe the limits of the Almighty?
> They are higher than the heavens—what can you do?
> They are deeper than the depths of the grave—what can you know?
> Their measure is longer than the earth and wider than the sea." Job 11:7-9

Mysticism, in its essence, transcends the constraints of thought and language, much like the nature of God. It not only invites us to explore the outermost limits of comprehension but also compels us to push beyond those boundaries. It is a profound summons to venture into realms that go beyond rationality, logic, and verifiable knowledge, extending even beyond the domains of theology, philosophy, and science. While some may perceive this as a mere flight of fancy, it is, in fact, an experience that countless individuals throughout human history have described as profoundly authentic, perhaps even more authentic, than the material world we often take for granted.

The very term 'mysticism' is closely tied to 'mystery'. It is an attempt to describe a relationship with Yahweh that is both hidden and revealed, known yet unknowable. The writings of saints and visionaries offer glimpses of this reality. You might experience a flicker of recognition in their words, a resonance that touches your innermost being. Yet the moment you try to translate this recognition into your own language, the experience splinters into paradoxes that leave you perplexed.

Pseudo-Dionysius, The Mystical Theology – "We pray that we may enter into the great darkness where, as scripture says, He truly dwells. What is most divine and most fitting is not to be known and not to be conceived."

MYSTICISM IS THE LIFESTYLE OF INEXPRESSIBLE UNION EXPRESSED IN RELATIONSHIP WITH JESUS

At its core, Christian mysticism revolves around cultivating a lifestyle of divine union unlocking the manifestation of Christ in you. However, even within this, the mystics recognise the profound unknowability of God. The question arises: How do you nurture a connection with something that transcends comprehension? Herein lies the paradox: the deeper you delve into the mystery of God, the more evident the limitations of human understanding become. Yet, it is through this very paradox that the beauty of Jesus emerges, allowing an inexpressible lifestyle to find expression through Him in you.

> Colossians 1:27 – "To them God has chosen to make known among the Gentiles the glorious riches of this mystery, which is Christ in you, the hope of glory."

Other mystical traditions, such as Buddhism or Taoism, approach the ineffable from different perspectives. In these systems, the concept of a personal God is often absent. This challenges the notion of mysticism as a strictly God experience. Even in Christian mysticism, where God is central, there remains the confounding reality of divine mystery. The language used to articulate God eventually dissolves into silence, as words cannot fully convey Him. However, it is important to note that Jesus is central to the mystical way as a believer, and he represents the adventure of journeying into the inexpressible mystery. Just as we cannot confine or control God, encountering Him in mystical experience produces equally untamable spirituality. What an adventure.

THE INADEQUACY OF LANGUAGE

Mystics have long accepted the inherent unknowability of divine encounters with God. However, giving up on the effort to understand mysticism means losing a chance to deepen your relationship with God and understand the mountain of your call in Him. Despite the inevitability of failure in fully articulating the mystical, the attempt itself holds value. By striving to describe the indescribable, we may catch fleeting glimpses of divine truth. Although mysticism eludes concrete definitions, the very act of engaging with it through language, silence, prayer, or contemplation becomes part of the journey.

We may falter in our efforts, but in that very faltering, grace abounds. The path of mysticism is not about achieving mastery or comprehension; it is about opening yourself to the mystery with humility and wonder. Mysticism invites you into a space where language fails, yet where meaning flourishes in silence beyond words. This ineffable encounter with Yahweh becomes a journey into the heart of mystery, an exploration of God's presence that transforms the mystic. Even as words falter, the heart may perceive a truth that language cannot convey.

The writings of mystics are filled with paradox, imagery, and silence, yet they are like signposts pointing toward a reality that lies just beyond the reach of expression and formation.

The Cloud of Unknowing (Anonymous, 14th century) — "For He may well be loved, but not thought. By love, He can be grasped and held, but by thought, never."

EMBRACING THE MYSTERY

To write about mysticism is to engage in a kind of sacred folly, knowing that complete success is impossible. Yet this very impossibility is part of the beauty. That's what I love about mysticism. It's the journey of pursuing the mystery revealed and protecting its hiddenness. I understand that this statement may be confusing, but the fundamental issue with mainstream Christianity is the loss of the sacredness of mystery. For the Christian, the assurance of grace accompanies the journey into divine mystery because failures and limitations of our language do not hinder God's presence. Rather, they remind us of our dependence on Him, whose reality surpasses all attempts at description. C'mon, is someone hearing this?

Mainstream Christianity has lost the art of the mystery, so we repackage what's mystery into the confines of what's acceptable and palatable at the price of authenticity.

Ultimately, the mystical path is one of surrender. It requires relinquishing the need to fully understand, define, or control the experience of God. This journey is characterised by a sense of awe, humility, and a readiness to embrace the mystery. Through this surrender, your soul awakens to the reality of God's tangible presence, even if that presence remains shrouded in mystery.

Mysticism, though impossible to capture, still beckons you to try. The act of trying is an act of faith, a response to God's invitation to delve deeper into the unknown. While language can never fully encapsulate this experience, it can serve as a companion on your journey, a tool for recollection, reflection, and prayer. Ultimately, mysticism is not about finding answers but about embracing the questions. It is about standing in the presence of the ineffable and allowing that encounter to shape and transform you.

> The mystery remains silent, yet it speaks to the depths of the spirit. And in that silent communion, we come to know a truth that goes beyond words.

The mystical pathway within Christianity is not separate from Jesus's core teachings...

The Journey Into Christian Mysticism: Hunger For Authenticity

At its heart, Christian mysticism represents an exciting journey into divine reality. It builds upon the revelatory teachings of Jesus, while also speaking to the deep spiritual longings of every generation. This mystical path offers a unique lens through which we can experience and understand the transformative power of divine love.

The modern world presents us with an unprecedented abundance of spiritual teachings and practices. Never before have believers had such ready access to diverse teachings of traditions, philosophies, and approaches to understanding God. Within this tapestry of spiritual wisdom, Christian mysticism stands out. It offers a distinctive approach rooted in the radical, non-confirmative Word which is Jesus, embracing the depths of contemplative practices and experiences.

THE FOUNDATION OF MYSTICAL CHRISTIANITY

The mystical pathway within Christianity is not separate from Jesus's core teachings; instead, it seeks to pursue a deeper engagement with them. Over the centuries, mystics have uncovered ways to illuminate and amplify these teachings, unveiling layers of meaning that directly address our innate yearning for divine connection and union. This rich pathway teaches how to transcend intellectual understanding of spiritual principles and enter direct, transformative experiences.

When we delve into concepts central to Christian spirituality, like repentance, holiness, prayer, and sacrifice, through a mystical lens, we uncover fresh interpretations that go beyond traditional religious boundaries. These concepts, which may bear difficult historical baggage or have been misused to inflict harm, gain new vitality when approached with contemplative awareness. By adopting a mystical perspective, we come to see these teachings not as rigid religious obligations but as invitations to enter into a more profound communion with divine reality. This unveiling opens up realms that lead us to ascend deeper into the original design and intention of who and what we are in Christ.

> Matthew 13:11 – "He answered them, 'To you it has been given to know the secrets of the kingdom of heaven, but to them it has not been given.'"

BRIDGING TRADITIONAL FAITH AND MYSTICAL EXPERIENCE

This might seem baffling to some, but here's a critical point to address: In many Christian circles, the elevation of the Bible inadvertently eclipses God himself. Bill Johnson quotes, "The Bible doesn't contain Jesus, but reveals Him." This is the essence of Christian mysticism. The Scriptures point to Christ, who is the true Rhema of the Logos, the living Word. They reveal the way to encounter Him rather than confining or limiting Him to the text.

Now let's wade into controversial waters. Many mystical believers have likely encountered the sceptical question: "Where's that in the Bible?" This question surfaces when trying to articulate a profound spiritual encounter or mystical experience to someone who approaches faith through the lens of traditional interpretation. How can a book truly encapsulate the infinite and transcendent aspects of countless spiritual experiences or encounters with divine entities?

Here's the reality: while the Bible holds unparalleled significance in Christian life, the ultimate authority is Jesus Christ, the Son of God. You might wonder, "what's the difference?" But the distinction is crucial. The Bible, as the inspired written word, serves as a compass and reference point for divine experiences. It helps us discern and align with the character, teachings, and divinity of Jesus. Christ, who is the way, the truth, and the life (John 14:6), however, remains the ultimate authority above all else.

Yes, the Scriptures are "God-breathed" (2 Timothy 3:16-17), but they are not the only source of divine inspiration.

> "All Scripture is God-breathed and is useful for teaching, rebuking, correcting and training in righteousness, so that the servant of God may be thoroughly equipped for every good work." (2 Timothy 3:16-17, NIV)

What constituted "all Scripture" within the early Church, prior to formal biblical canonisation? For early believers, "Scripture" encompassed the Hebrew manuscripts (Old Testament) and a range of other sacred texts. Some of these, like the Dead Sea Scrolls, the Book of Enoch, and the Book of Jasher and other apocryphal books, held significant influence. Other mystical texts later on, such as the Zohar and the Sefer Yetzirah, explored divine mysteries with great depth and insight.

Although not universally accepted as canonical, these writings offer layers of spiritual insight. The key is not to view the Bible as a restrictive boundary but as a beacon that helps us remain true to the moral character and divine revelation of Jesus. Christian mysticism acknowledges that discernment, wisdom, and spiritual maturity are essential when engaging with these texts. Not all extra-biblical writings are accurate, and that's precisely the beauty of the mystical path. It empowers believers to test and discard what conflicts with biblical truth, recognising that we are no longer bound by the rigid confines of spiritual infancy. We are not toddlers; we are sons of God. We are part of the remnant, not the empire.

> John 21:25 (NKJV)
>
> "And there are also many other things that Jesus did, which, if they were written one by one, I suppose that even the world itself could not contain the books that would be written."
>
> 2 Peter 1:20-21 (NIV)
>
> "Above all, you must understand that no prophecy of Scripture came about by the prophet's own interpretation of things. For prophecy never had its origin in the human will, but prophets, though human, spoke from God as they were carried along by the Holy Spirit."

The prophetic experience did not cease with the closing of the canon. As believers, called to be kings, priests, and prophets after the order of Melchizedek, we continue to receive divine revelations. The Holy Spirit gives spiritual "downloads", insights, visions, and encounters that transcend what is documented in Biblical Scripture. While the Bible may not document many of these experiences and encounters, we use Biblical scripture as our plumb line to ensure our mystical encounters reflect the moral character and divinity of Jesus, as revealed in scripture.

Christian mystics are not seeking to forge a new theology. Instead, they endeavour to restore the authenticity and purity of a lifestyle, a return to the primordial state of intimate communion with God. This journey is not always easy. It will challenge established norms, provoke scepticism, and ruffle feathers. But it is a journey worth embracing, a journey of transformative faith that seeks the living God beyond the confines of ink and paper through direct encounter and unwavering devotion.

Prepare yourself for this journey. Your words, actions, and methods may unsettle those who are content with surface-level faith, but you are called to a deeper reality. Embrace the mystical path with confidence, knowing that it leads not away from Christ but into His very heart.

The Constantinian shift had a profound impact on Christian thought and spirituality...

The Influence Of Constantine The Great...Or Was He...

Emperor Constantine: Architect of a New Christian World and His 'UNFORTUNATE' Enduring Impact on the Church and the Bible

CONSTANTINE IN CONTEXT

In the annals of history, few figures have left as indelible a mark on Christianity as Emperor Constantine (272-337 AD). His ascent to power and subsequent patronage of the Christian faith transformed a marginalised sect into a force that would shape Western civilisation for centuries. That might sound positive to you… but it had it's short comings. Constantine's reign did not merely legitimise Christianity; it profoundly altered the Church's structure, theology, and even the way the sacred texts were understood and disseminated.

The early church differed significantly from the modern concept of a church. One key distinction is the characteristics that set a sect apart from a cult. In a cult, a single leader typically holds dictatorial power, with their words and actions being treated as law and scripture by followers. In contrast, a sect comprises individuals who have broken away from a dominant system while remaining true to its source. The early church was viewed as a sect, functioning autonomously and free from external control or hierarchy. However, this independence was viewed unfavourably by the Roman Empire, ultimately prompting Constantine's entrance and influence.

Before Constantine, the Christian Church faced centuries of persecution under the Roman Empire. Believers were forced to meet in secret, preserving their faith under the threat of torture and death. The early Church was decentralised, diverse in practice and belief, and bound by shared devotion in mystical practices rather than a rigid institutional framework. Constantine's embrace of Christianity was not simply a political manoeuvre but a watershed event that altered the dynamics between faith and empire, secular and sacred power.

CONSTANTINE'S CONVERSION AND THE VISION OF THE CROSS

Constantine's conversion from a pagan ruler to a Christian emperor is a highly debated historical event. The turning point happened in 312 AD, just before the Battle of the Milvian Bridge. As per Eusebius of Caesarea, Constantine had a vision where a cross of light appeared in the sky bearing the words "In hoc signo vinces" ("In this sign, you will conquer"). Later that night, it would seem that Christ appeared to Constantine in a dream, instructing him to adopt the cross as his symbol in battle.

Constantine's victory the next day secured his control over the Western Roman Empire, and he attributed his success to the Christian God. This moment symbolised the convergence of divine favour and political power, a synthesis that would become a hallmark of Constantine's reign. His conversion was genuine, though complex. Constantine kept aspects of pagan symbolism throughout his life, but his favour toward Christianity was transformative for the faith.

THE EDICT OF MILAN: THE LEGALISATION OF CHRISTIANITY

In 313 AD, Constantine, alongside his co-emperor Licinius, issued the Edict of Milan. This decree granted religious tolerance throughout the Roman Empire, effectively legalising Christianity. The Edict was not merely an act of mercy; it was a strategic acknowledgement of Christianity's growing influence. For Christians, this was nothing short of miraculous. Churches were built, public worship was instituted, and confiscated properties were returned. Constantine's patronage went beyond mere tolerance. He provided financial support for the construction of grand basilicas, such as the Church of the Holy Sepulchre in Jerusalem and the original St. Peter's Basilica in Rome. The Church was no longer a clandestine movement; it had the emperor's blessing and resources. This, however, was exactly the problem. In one edict, the freedom and authenticity of the Christian faith, its gatherings, theology of the Word, and freedom were suppressed, coming under the control of an empire threatened by the freedom and expansion of a radically expanding faith. Christianity, considered a sect, did not conform to the constructs and oppression of control. It remained free, even under persecution, and the Roman Empire knew it.

CONSTANTINE AND THE COUNCIL OF NICAEA

Constantine's most lasting impact on Christian history is often attributed to his organisation of the First Council of Nicaea in 325 AD. At that time, the Church, now officially acknowledged, was grappling with internal rifts stemming from theological disagreements, most notably the Arian Controversy. Arius, a priest from Alexandria, contended that Jesus Christ was a creation of God the Father and therefore not co-eternal or of the same substance as Him. This contradicted the emerging orthodox belief in the Trinity. In a bid for unity across his empire, Constantine summoned bishops from various Christian regions to resolve the issue. The Council of Nicaea led to the formulation of the Nicene Creed, which affirmed Christ's divinity and proclaimed Him to be "of the same substance" as the Father. The creed established the foundation for Christian orthodoxy and discredited Arianism as a heresy. While this was a positive development, the influence over theology extended beyond, leading to a more rational approach that expanded dogma and theology while reducing the mystery of the mystical and personal experience.

Though Constantine was not a theologian himself, his influence on the council was substantial. He presided over the meetings and made sure that the decisions taken were supported by imperial authority. This fusion of imperial power and theological doctrine represented a pivotal moment, as Christianity became closely linked to the structures of the empire. Are you taking notes?... CHRISTIANITY TRANSFORMED FROM BEING AUTHENTIC AND FREE TO CATASTROPHICALLY ALIGNING WITH A STRUCTURE OF CONTROL.

CONSTANTINE AND THE FORMATION OF THE BIBLICAL CANON

The question of the biblical canon, what texts should be considered authoritative Scripture, was another issue that gained momentum during Constantine's reign. While Constantine did not directly determine the canon, his support of the Church facilitated formalising the texts that would become the Bible. Under Constantine's orders, the scholar and bishop Eusebius of Caesarea was commissioned to produce fifty copies of the Scriptures for the churches in Constantinople, the new Christian capital of the empire. This project necessitated selecting which books would be included, contributing to the crystallisation of the canon. Though debates about certain books continued, Constantine's initiative accelerated the process of consensus…in other words…Constantine will have the final say.

Constantine's endorsement of the Church's leaders meant that their theological decisions carried the weight of imperial approval. The canonisation process, therefore, was not solely grassroots spiritual discernment but became an endeavour undergirded by imperial order, and that order came with control.

THE TRANSFORMATION OF THE CHURCH: FROM PERSECUTED SECT TO IMPERIAL INSTITUTION

Constantine's influence fundamentally changed the character of the Church. Before his reign, Christians saw themselves as a counter-cultural community, committed to a faith that often stood in opposition to the Roman state and its framework. Martyrdom was a testament of faithfulness, and the teachings of early mystics and church fathers emphasised spiritual purity and separation from worldly systems. It was a deeply authentic faith, overflowing with spiritual power and centred on unity and ecstasy in Christ. Experiences of ecstasy were marked by rapturous moments, ascensions, and out-of-body experiences that surpassed rational thought or behaviour. Within the Christian community, freedom in the spirit was tangible.

With Constantine's patronage, the Church gained wealth, status, and political influence. Bishops began to function as imperial administrators, adjudicating disputes and managing vast resources. The humility of the early Church gave way to the grandeur of imperial-sponsored liturgy and architecture. Not everyone welcomed this transformation. Some Christian mystics like St. Anthony the Great and St. Pachomius viewed the new alignment with the empire as a threat to the Church's spiritual integrity.

CONSTANTINE'S LEGACY: UNITY AND COMPROMISE

Constantine's impact on Christianity was paradoxical. On one hand, he provided stability, unity, and legitimacy to a persecuted faith. He protected Christians from violence, elevated their leaders, and facilitated the spread of Christian doctrine and Scripture. The Nicene Creed and the developing canon of the Bible owed much to his influence. On the other hand, his reign introduced compromises between faith and structural power. The Church's association with imperial authority led to new challenges, including corruption, political control and power. The simplicity and mystical teachings of Jesus and the early apostles now had to coexist with the grandeur of the empire.

The Constantinian shift had a profound impact on Christian thought and spirituality, with tensions introduced by Constantine's legacy persisting throughout history. The medieval Church faced challenges in balancing spiritual authority and temporal power, while the Reformation later questioned the concept of state-supported Christianity, aiming for a revival of a more apostolic faith. In conclusion, Constantine's legacy continues to endure.

Emperor Constantine's rule marked a pivotal moment for Christianity. He reshaped an organic movement of the Ekklesia into a formal institution, shaping the evolution of doctrine, the Scripture canon, and the dynamics between the Church and the state. His legacy weaves together elements of faith and politics.

Constantine's conversion was authentic, but his vision for the Church was closely linked to his vision for the empire. The victory of the cross at the Milvian Bridge brought both blessing and curse. The Church, no longer facing persecution, yet found its freedom restricted by a framework that mirrored the empire's structure of control. This conformity deprived the church of its authenticity and influence it enjoyed as an Ekklesia, free to express its faith and mystical practices.

..there is a new Ekklesia rising, unlocking the ancient paths...

Mysticism and
Spirituality

Many Christians view 'spirituality' as the embodiment of their faith through personal or communal practices. These practices can manifest in various ways, such as prayer, Bible study, ethical living, participation in devotional traditions, engagement in charismatic prayer meetings, attending revivals, or regularly worshipping on Sundays. These significant dimensions of Christian spirituality are deeply valued by believers.

However, Christian mysticism stands apart within the realm of traditional spirituality. While spirituality encompasses the lived experience of faith, mystics dedicate themselves to exploring the depths of the mystery of sonship to govern and co create with

Yahweh, and the dynamic interplay of a contemplative lifestyle. Mysticism beckons believers to an encounter that surpasses the surface level of religious practice. This invitation doesn't merely enhance spiritual life; it plunges believers into unknown depths where they surrender understanding to God's transforming power, unveiling Christ's mystical position within and revealing God's sons as the microcosms of the macrocosm.

In contrast to certain expressions of spirituality that may reinforce traditional identity, mysticism demands the opposite. It calls for a courageous and humble relinquishment of self before the enigmatic nature of the cross. This journey necessitates embracing uncertainty; medieval Christian mysticism calls this the "cloud of unknowing," where reason submits to faith. Similarly, mysticism may guide you through spiritual desolation, shedding preconceived ideas, and ultimately leading you into a profound entanglement with the image of God. Mysticism is not about striving but about letting go and aligning yourself with His rhythm, allowing the revealed mystery to unfold.

Not everyone is attracted to this esoteric path, and most likely because of misconceptions. Many faithful people may find comfort and purpose in simpler expressions of their faith. For some, faith is a journey of quiet contemplation and spiritual wonder; for others, it's expressed through simple, observable acts of worship, devotion, and service. That being said, once you're a mystic, you're always a mystic. It's impossible to describe the intoxicating blend of depth, bliss, and connection offered by this lifestyle; once experienced, a return to traditional, and let's be honest, conventional ways of spirituality is unthinkable.

A word of warning here: The diversity in spiritual experiences reflects the vastness of God's grace. The community of believers includes those who pursue the hidden path of mystical union and those who live their faith in straightforward, practical ways. Each path is valid, and neither is superior to the other. Jesus's admonition to "judge not" serves as a reminder that the authenticity of someone's faith journey is not for us to evaluate. Each person's spiritual path unfolds uniquely, and we are called to respect and honour these differences.

I believe with all my heart that there is a massive shifting in the spirit taking place, sifting through practices and programs, returning the sons of God to their original intent. The 20th-century theologian Karl Rahner said, **"The Christian of the future will be a mystic or will not exist at all."** This statement suggests that as Christianity faces the challenges of an increasingly secular world, a return to the heart of divine mystery will be essential for its vitality. The Spirit is already moving in this direction, calling more believers to embrace a contemplative, mystical awareness that can transform the entire body of Christ into a more deeply unified, spiritual community. The modern framework of charismatic, evangelical and denominational factions are not a beautiful picture of diversity but rather division, a Christian faith that cannot agree upon its own theology.

Mysticism often operates quietly, hidden within the rhythms of ordinary life. It is woven into the fabric of Scripture, where stories of divine encounter invite us to go beyond the literal and enter into the mystery. Any moment of prayer, stillness, or longing for God can become an opening to the mystical dimension. Yet, this path is not something that can be handed to us effortlessly; it must be sought with intentionality and openness.

Bernard McGinn, a scholar of Christian mysticism, reflected on the insights of William of St. Thierry, a medieval mystic, who described the journey of seeing God not as a literal vision but as an inner transformation through grace and faith. According to William, "Seeing God begins with a vision that is not a vision, but God's invisible presence working within us by grace." This gradual development of the capacity to "see" God is synonymous with growing in love for God. The more we are transformed by divine love, the more we come to know and experience God's presence. In this sense, the mystical journey is not about extraordinary experiences but about becoming more deeply united with God, to the point that one's very being reflects the divine. The mirroring.

The journey into mysticism is, in many ways, a journey home—to the heart of God, where all striving ceases and one is simply held in divine love. It is a path that may challenge, purify, and transform. But it is a path worth walking, for in embracing the mystery, we find the fullness of life that Jesus promised. Whether you are just beginning this journey or have travelled far, the mystic lifestyle leeds forever deeper into the mystery of the ecstasy of God's love.

> Luke 17:20-21 – "The kingdom of God is not coming with signs to be observed, nor will they say, 'Look, here it is!' or 'There!' for behold, the kingdom of God is within you."

WHAT IS A MYSTIC?

> Pseudo-Dionysius, The Mystical Theology –"The more we climb, the more our speech falls silent, for we move into the realm of the Ineffable, where all knowing ceases."

A mystic is someone who traverses the ancient paths where heaven and earth intersect, delving deeper into the mystical chambers of Yahweh's presence. These individuals have had their hearts pierced by the radiant love of Jesus, and their lives have been transformed by the wisdom that emanates from their union and ecstasy with Christ. Being a mystic does not involve forsaking the world for abstraction; rather, it entails bearing witness to the sacred unfolding of mystery within everyday life. It means perceiving the burning bush concealed within the gentle movements of the Spirit in the pauses between words.

True mysticism is not an escape from reality but an awakening to its deeper currents. It is the unveiling of our oneness with Christ, the revelation that the Cross is not merely a historical event of salvation from damnation but a doorway into divine participation. Mystics are those who have learned to dwell on this threshold, to live in the crossing between heaven's light and earth's shadow, allowing the power of divine love to shape their being.

Yet many mistakenly believe that mysticism belongs only to the East, that Christian mysticism is a borrowed light, a fusion of Hindu or Buddhist practices with Christian language. Such a view is not only misguided but also blind to the wellspring of mystical wisdom woven into biblical faith. The Christian mystical path is deeply rooted in Hebrew scripture, in the prophetic traditions, in the sacred wisdom of Jewish sages, and above all, in Jesus—the ultimate mystic, whose life was the perfect embodiment of divine oneness. The Gospel is, at its heart, a mystical revelation: an invitation to abide in the hidden mystery of God, where eternity bends to kiss the finite.

Christian mysticism offers not a philosophy nor an intellectual ascent but a path—a way of being drawn into the divine embrace. It is an ecstatic reality, one that entangles mystical knowledge and esoteric practices with a heart attuned to the whispering breath of the Spirit. Yet, as the soul deepens in this sacred journey, hidden realities unfold, and mysteries once obscured emerge into the light. This is the way of divine transformation: not a riddle to be solved, but an ever-deepening participation in the Love that holds all things together.

A mystic is one who has glimpsed the unseen architecture of reality, who has tasted the eternal in the temporal, and who now seeks to walk in harmony with that mystery. Through contemplation, prayer, and surrender, they attune themselves to the ecstasy of the current, seeking not to understand but to become—to embody the sacred entanglement of human and divine, where the Word becomes flesh anew in the soul's sanctuary.

The very term "mystic" is drawn from the Greek mystikos (μυστικός), meaning "hidden" or "secret," a fitting reflection of the ineffable nature of the Divine. Yet this concept is not foreign to the biblical truth; the Hebrew scriptures, too, speak of the hidden mysteries of God. The word Sod (סוֹד) denotes the secret counsels of Yahweh, truths veiled from the unready yet unveiled to the righteous. As the Psalmist declares, "The secret (סוֹד) of the Lord is with those who fear Him" (Psalm 25:14). Similarly, Nistar (נִסְתָּר), meaning "hidden" or "concealed," points to realities that lie beyond the grasp of human perception, known only through divine revelation. "The hidden things belong to the Lord our God" (Deuteronomy 29:29)—yet what is hidden is not hidden forever but awaits the moment of unveiling.

In the New Testament, this theme resounds through the

writings of Paul, who speaks of the mystērion (μυστήριον), the sacred mystery now revealed in Christ. "The mystery (μυστήριον) that has been hidden for ages and generations is now revealed to His saints" (Colossians 1:26). This is the great unveiling: that Christ, the Eternal Logos, now dwells within us, "the hope of glory" (Colossians 1:27). No longer is God's presence locked away in the Holy of Holies; the veil is torn, and the sacred fire now burns within the human heart.

The mystic stands at this threshold between concealment and revelation, between the seen and the unseen. They are those who have learned to see with the eye of the heart, to hear the silent speech of God echoing in the depths of the soul. For, as Paul writes,

> "What has been concealed for ages in a realm inaccessible to the senses, what no eye has seen, nor ear heard, nor human mind conceived—this God has already arranged and is now revealing by His Spirit," (1 Corinthians 2:9-10, Mirror Translation).

Here lies the essence of Christian mysticism: the realisation that the "secret things" of God are not veiled but revealed, not inaccessible but hidden only until the soul is ready to see. The mysteries of the Kingdom are not puzzles to be solved but invitations to deeper union, calling us ever further into the radiant depths of divine love and the ecstasy of mystery.

To walk the mystical path is to enter this unfolding revelation, to live within the paradox of hiddenness and unveiling, presence, and mystery. It is to stand, like Moses before the burning bush, in the presence of the inexpressible.

THE ORIGINS OF CHRISTIAN MYSTICISM

The luminous thread of Christian mysticism, though traced by scholars such as Evelyn Underhill, Rowan Williams, and Bernard McGinn, is woven from strands both seen and unseen. Its roots do not lie in intellectual reflection but in the deep, living currents of spiritual experience, currents that move beneath history's surface, shaping the inner life of those drawn to Divine entanglement. This mystical way is no late bloom upon the tree of Christian faith but an ancient reality, flowing from three profound wellsprings: the sacred Hebrew language and letters, the contemplative wisdom of Greek thought, and the revelatory presence of Christ.

JESUS AND THE EARLY CHRISTIAN MYSTICS

At the heart of Christian mysticism stands Jesus Christ, not just as a teacher of wisdom but as the embodied threshold between the temporal and the eternal. His words, veiled in parable and paradox, hint at realities beyond expression. His life, marked by moments of profound spiritual intimacy, his desert solitude, his nights spent in prayer, his transfiguration upon the mount manifests the mystery of divine communion. The invitation to "abide in Me" reveals an ecstasy of participation in God's life, a deeply mystical experience. Jesus is the embodiment of mysticism. His closest disciples glimpsed this mystery and sought to articulate it in their own language of light and union.

MYSTICISM IN EARLY CHRISTIAN THOUGHT AND PRACTICE

Yet the mystical path is not grasped all at once. It unfolds, deepening over centuries, finding expression not only in direct experience but in reflection, ecstasy, and the slow ripening of intimacy. The first centuries of Christianity saw the birth of mystical theology, a way of knowing that embraces the unknowing, recognising that the God is too vast for human speech to contain. The early Church, in calling its sacraments mysteria, acknowledged this hiddenness, the Eucharist, for instance, was not merely a ritual but a veil through which divine mystery shone.

It was within the barren landscapes of the desert that Christian mysticism took on a new intensity. The Desert Fathers and Mothers, drawn by a hunger for God that the world could not satisfy, abandoned the cities and sought the wilderness. In silence and solitude, they plumbed the depths of the soul, battling inner struggles and awakening to divine presence in the stillness. Anthony the Great, Syncletica of Alexandria, and their kin in asceticism discovered that the path to God is one of purification, a stripping away of illusion, a refining of the heart until it becomes transparent to divine light.

In the distant isles of the Celtic lands, another strain of Christian mysticism emerged, one attuned to the whisper of God in wind and wave, the sacred fire that burns in both stone and soul. Saints such as Brigid of Kildare and Columba of Iona lived with a profound awareness of the numinous presence in all things, seeing no divide between the material and the spiritual. Their prayers and poetry reflect a vision in which the wild, untamed beauty of creation speaks of the eternal, where heaven and earth are not separate realms but overlapping realities.

THE FLOWERING OF MEDIEVAL MYSTICISM

If the early centuries planted the seeds, it was in the Middle Ages that Christian mysticism burst into full bloom, unfurling in the writings of visionaries, poets, and saints. Julian of Norwich, John of the Cross, and Teresa of Ávila poured forth revelations of divine love, of the soul's longing and the dark night of purification, of the ecstasy and fire that mark the way of union with God. Their words are not theoretical, they are born of encounter, of wounds transfigured into wisdom, of hearts set ablaze.

Yet this flowering was not an isolated occurrence. It grew from the deep roots of scripture, the contemplative practices of the early Church, and the spiritual architectures built by generations of mystics who walked the hidden path before them. They drew from the same wellsprings, the Hebrew prophets who saw visions of the ineffable, and the soul's ascent, and above all, the living mystery of Christ, in whom all things are gathered into one.

A TRADITION OF UNFOLDING MYSTERY

The origins of Christian mysticism are not fixed points in history but an ever-flowing stream, fed by the deep wells of Jewish and Hebrew mystery, Greek wisdom, and the burning presence of

Christ. To follow this stream is not necessarily to study the past but to step into the current, to recognise that the mystical path is not the possession of scholars or saints alone but remains open to any who dare to seek the mystery within. It is a path of unknowing and illumination, of silence and song, of surrender and transformation, a journey into the vast and luminous mystery of God.

...there is a massive shifting in the spirit taking place...

The Jewish Foundations of Christian Mysticism

John 4:22 – "You worship what you do not know; we worship what we know, for salvation is from the Jews."

Christianity and Judaism are bound together by an ancient and sacred lineage, yet their relationship has often been clouded by misunderstanding. Christianity did not arise in isolation; it sprang from the mystical wellspring of Jewish/Hebrew spirituality—the faith that Jesus and his earliest followers lived and breathed. To grasp the full splendour of Christian mysticism, one must first gaze into the luminous depths of Judaism's own contemplative heritage. Yet, history has often cast a veil over this truth, portraying Judaism as a rigid legalism from which Jesus sought to liberate his disciples. Such a view, however, is born of a dim and narrow reading of both Jewish heritage and Jesus's life and teachings. By returning with open hearts and unclouded vision to the mystical currents of Judaism, we unearth a wisdom that shaped early Christianity and continues to whisper its secrets today.

> Romans 11:17-18 – "But if some of the branches were broken off, and you, although a wild olive shoot, were grafted in among the others and now share in the nourishing root of the olive tree, do not be arrogant toward the branches. If you are, remember it is not you who support the root, but the root that supports you."

THE ESSENCE OF JEWISH MYSTICISM

Judaism is no mere framework of laws and customs; it is a living, breathing quest for divine encounter, a tradition shimmering with the fire of revelation. At its core, it pulses with the longing to behold the face of God and to be transformed in that beholding. This is the world from which Jesus emerged and the soil in which the earliest Christian communities took root.

When one speaks of "Jewish mysticism," the mind may leap first to Kabbalah. Kabbalistic insights have indeed rippled outward, leaving their imprint on Christian mystics like Teresa of Ávila and Luis de León.

Kabbalah, the mystical tradition within Judaism, is an esoteric system of spiritual wisdom that seeks to understand the nature of God, creation, and the soul. Its name comes from the Hebrew root QBL (קבל), meaning "to receive," signifying both the transmission of sacred knowledge and the reception of divine truths and mysteries that transcend human intellect. Kabbalah is not merely a philosophical or theological system but a dynamic path of spiritual insight and transformation that aims to entangle your heart with divinity. As Christians, we find ourselves in Christ and Christ in us.

Instead of striving to draw nearer to God, we now embrace the journey and engage in mystical practices that reveal the oneness and unity we experience through our divine entanglement with Him.

ORIGINS AND EARLY DEVELOPMENT

The origins of Kabbalah are shrouded in mystery, with roots extending deep into the biblical and Rabbinic traditions of Judaism. Many Kabbalists trace their lineage to the mystical visions found in the Hebrew Bible, particularly the prophetic experiences of figures like Ezekiel and Isaiah. The Merkavah ("Chariot") mysticism of the early centuries CE, which sought to comprehend the divine throne seen in Ezekiel's visions, laid the groundwork for later Kabbalistic thought.

During the medieval period, Kabbalah emerged as a more structured and profound mystical tradition. The 12th and 13th centuries saw the rise of seminal texts such as the Sefer ha-Bahir ("Book of Brightness") and Sefer Yetzirah ("Book of Creation"), which introduced key concepts like the Sefirot—ten emanations of divine energy through which God interacted to unfold creation. The most influential Kabbalistic text, the Zohar ("Book of Splendor"), traditionally attributed to Rabbi Shimon bar Yochai but more likely compiled by the Spanish mystic Moses de León in the 13th century, offers a vast and poetic exposition of the mystical dimensions of Torah, creation, and the human soul.

CORE CONCEPTS OF KABBALAH

At the heart of Kabbalah is the idea that the visible world is only a fraction of reality. Beyond it lies a spiritual cosmos structured through divine emanations. The Sefirot, arranged in a mystical diagram known as the Tree of Life, serve as channels through which divine light flows from the infinite source, Ein Sof ("The Infinite"), into the created world. These ten attributes not only describe aspects of God but also correspond to dimensions of human consciousness and ethical development. More on this topic later.

MYSTICISM AND THE PATH TO GOD

Kabbalah seeks direct experiential knowledge of God. Techniques such as meditation, permutations of divine names, and deep contemplative study of Torah enable the mystic to ascend through spiritual worlds. At its highest level, Kabbalah offers the possibility of mystical union (devekut), in which the soul cleaves to Yahweh in ecstatic oneness.

Kabbalah is, therefore, not merely a body of knowledge but a transformative journey—one that reveals the hidden dimensions of existence and aligns the mystic with the cosmic order of divine wisdom.

THE HEBREW SCRIPTURES: THE WELLSPRING OF MYSTICAL THOUGHT

Yet, the roots of Jewish mysticism run deeper than Kabbalah, stretching into the sacred texts of the Hebrew Scriptures—the Tanakh, the lifeblood of both Jewish and Christian spirituality. These ancient writings are not just historical accounts but portals to divine encounter, where prophecy, vision, and transformation unfold within the seeker

In I Samuel 10:6, the prophet Samuel declares to Saul: "Then the Spirit of the Lord will rush upon you, and you will prophesy with them, and you will be transformed into another man." This moment encapsulates the very heart of mystical experience, an overwhelming descent of the divine Spirit, an ecstatic awakening, and a radical transfiguration of the self. The "Spirit of the Lord," the Ruach Yahweh, foreshadows what Christians would later know as the Holy Spirit. Here, Judaism reveals itself not as a dry system of laws but as a living path of divine encounter, one that is fiery, ecstatic, and intimately personal.

VISIONS AND THEOPHANIES: ENCOUNTERS WITH THE DIVINE

Throughout the Hebrew Scriptures, the veil between heaven and earth grows thin. Time and again, mortals are drawn into direct encounters with God, moments where eternity pierces through the temporal:

Moses and the Burning Bush – A voice from within the flames, a divine call issuing from the heart of mystery.

Elijah's Encounter with God – Not in the wind, nor the earthquake, nor the fire, but in the "sheer silence" (1 Kings 19:12).

Isaiah's Vision of Divine Glory – The temple quakes, the seraphim cry "Holy, Holy, Holy," and the prophet is undone (Isaiah 6).

Ezekiel's vision of the Chariot – Wheels within wheels, living creatures flashing like fire, and the throne of sapphire above them (Ezekiel 1).

Ezekiel's vision, known as Merkavah mysticism, became the foundation for early Jewish mystical ascent, later recorded in the Hekhalot literature, which describes soul journeys into the palatial realms of God. Here, we find striking parallels with early Christian thought: Jesus's ascension, Paul's journey to the "third heaven" (2 Corinthians 12:2), and the mystical ascent of later Christian contemplatives. These encounters reveal an enduring truth—that the human soul, drawn by divine love, always yearns to ascend, to pierce beyond the veil, to see and be transformed.

MEDITATION AND CONTEMPLATION: SHARED MYSTICAL PRACTICES

Mysticism is not only vision, it is also stillness, the turning inward to hear the whisper of God. Jewish mysticism, like its Christian counterpart, is steeped in contemplative practice, where scripture is not merely read but inhabited, pondered with the heart until its hidden light unfolds.

Twentieth-century Kabbalistic scholar Aryeh Kaplan unearthed this contemplative dimension within the Hebrew Bible, revealing it to be not just a book of law but a guide to mystical meditation. In Meditation and the Bible, he reimagines Psalm 119:15: "I will meditate on Your precepts and gaze upon Your ways," reinterpreted as "In Your mysteries I will meditate, and I will gaze upon Your paths." The shift is subtle yet profound—what was once mere moral instruction becomes an invitation into divine mystery.

Kaplan delineates a journey through contemplation: from distraction into stillness, from stillness into luminous silence, from silence into encounter. Elijah's wind, earthquake, and fire mirror the turbulence of the mind, yet beyond them lies the whisper of God. This path, so vividly present in Jewish mysticism, finds its echo in Christian traditions—from the Hesychastic prayer of the Eastern Church to the silent surrender of The Cloud of Unknowing.

SILENCE AND STILLNESS: THE LANGUAGE OF DIVINE ENCOUNTER

In both paths, silence is not emptiness but fullness, the language in which God speaks most profoundly. The Psalms, so central to both Jewish and Christian devotion, resound with this wisdom:

> "Be still and know that I am God." (Psalm 46:10)

> "For God alone, my soul waits in silence." (Psalm 62:1)

> "To You, silence is praise, O God." (Psalm 65:1)

For the mystic, silence is not absence but presence, the pregnant hush in which Yahweh makes Himself known. The Christian contemplative reinterprets Habakkuk's words—"The Lord is in His holy temple; let all the earth be silent before Him" (Habakkuk 2:20)—as an inner reality: the heart itself becomes the temple, and silence its sacred space.

THE MYSTICAL PATH: FROM PURIFICATION TO UNION

Early Christian theologian Origen saw in the Hebrew Scriptures a blueprint for the mystical journey:

Proverbs—the path of purification, where discipline and wisdom cleanse the soul.

Ecclesiastes—the path of illumination, where deeper understanding leads beyond the illusions of the world.

The Song of Songs—the path of union, where the soul, like the bride, longs for the Divine Bridegroom.

This journey, deeply rooted in Jewish wisdom, finds its full flowering in Christian mysticism, where the soul is drawn ever deeper into the fire of divine love in Christ.

THE LIBERATING LOVE OF GOD

At the heart of Jewish and Christian mysticism alike is not constraint, but freedom, the Exodus of the soul from the bondage of tradition into the vastness of divine love. The ancient liberation from Egypt mirrors the soul's own journey, a passage from fear and separation into the embrace of the Infinite.

Yet this journey is not for the few but for all. The Spirit moves where it wills, stirring in the hearts of all who seek. In rediscovering the Jewish roots of Christian mysticism, we reclaim an ancient kinship—a shared longing, a common quest for the One who is beyond and yet within, the Eternal Mystery whose face we seek.

For in the end, to entangle with the oneness of God is the essence of all true mysticism—Jewish, Christian, and beyond.

*...mysticism
provided a way
of articulating
the soul's journey
toward divine union*

The Greek
Contribution

The word mysticism is a relatively modern construct, emerging in the early 18th century. It first entered the English language in 1700, long after the foundational texts of Christian theology and the philosophical writings of ancient Greece were set down. Yet while the term itself is new, the experience it describes is ancient, woven into the fabric of human longing for the Divine. To grasp how mysticism, especially the pursuit of divine union, took shape, we must turn to the Greek origins of its name. The root verb 'mueo' μυέω means "to close" or "to shut," evoking the act of veiling the eyes or sealing the lips, turning inward for the divine revealing and manifestation of the ecstasy of mystery.

French theologian Louis Bouyer, in his seminal work Mysticism: An Essay on the History of the Word, draws attention to this imagery of closure. To close the eyes signifies an inward turning—a deliberate withdrawal from the distractions of the outer world into the depths of the soul. To seal the lips suggests a discipline of silence, a reverent listening before one dares to speak of the ineffable. Yet 'mueo' holds another meaning: initiation. It denotes a passage into concealed knowledge, an unveiling of realities hidden from the unprepared.

This theme of initiation was central to the mystery religions of ancient Greece, traditions shrouded in secrecy, yet rich with transformative power. These were not mere cultic observances; they were pathways of metamorphosis, each devoted to a deity whose myth carried the weight of cosmic truth. The Orphic mysteries revolved around Orpheus, who journeyed into the underworld seeking to retrieve his lost Eurydice, while the Eleusinian mysteries honoured Demeter and Persephone, whose descent into darkness and return to light mirrored the rhythms of death and rebirth.

The symbolism of these underworld journeys is profound, offering a lens through which the mystical path can be understood. They speak of descent into the hidden places of the soul, where surface realities dissolve and a deeper truth is encountered. Initiation into these mysteries was not a matter of intellectual grasp but of lived experience, an embodied encounter with the sacred. What precisely transpired within these rites remains unknown, for silence was part of the transmission. Yet we can discern their essence: they transformed consciousness to lead the mystic beyond mere belief into the direct apprehension of God.

Bouyer suggests that what was guarded in secrecy was not esoteric doctrine but the rites themselves, the sacred gestures, symbols, and moments of encounter. The power of these rituals lay not in the words that described them but in the transformation they enacted. In this, the Greek mysteries prefigured the mystical impulse that would later find expression within Christianity: an encounter with divinity that is not merely understood but undergone.

FROM PAGAN MYSTERIES TO CHRISTIAN REVELATION

As Christianity took root in the Greco-Roman world, it encountered and reinterpreted this legacy of mystery. The early Church did not adopt the secretive rites of the pagan traditions, yet it recognised in them a language well-suited to the unveiling of divine truths. The apostle Paul himself frequently employs the term mysterion, speaking of sacred realities once hidden but now disclosed through Christ.

Yet there is a striking reversal. Whereas the mysteries of old were accessible only to a chosen few, the Christian mystery was proclaimed to all. The hidden things of God were not locked away in secret chambers but were revealed in the life, death, and resurrection of Jesus. Paul speaks of "the mystery hidden for ages and generations, but now revealed to his saints" (Colossians 1:26). This is not a secret jealously guarded, but a truth unveiled—a call to all who would seek a divine union.

Yet, paradoxically, even as the Gospel unveils, it also conceals. Christian mysticism is not a single moment of revelation but a dynamic, unfolding journey of the ancient paths. The fullness of divine union is not grasped all at once; it beckons, ever deeper, into mystery. The Greek contribution to Christian thought lies in this tension between hiddenness and disclosure, a tension that compels you to move beyond surface knowledge into the depths of divine reality.

THE TRANSFORMATIVE NATURE OF CHRISTIAN MYSTICISM

The Greek concept of mystery, with its themes of initiation and transformation, resonated deeply with the early Christian experience. Baptism, for instance, was more than a ritual of cleansing; it was a rite of passage, a death to the old self and rebirth into the divine life of Christ. The Eucharist (or known as communion), too, carried mystical significance, not as a mere remembrance but as a direct participation in the body and blood of Christ, an entry into sacred union.

Early Christian thinkers such as Clement of Alexandria and Origen drew upon the language of mystery to articulate the soul's journey toward God. For them, the Christian life was not static belief but progressive illumination. Clement described a spiritual ascent, beginning with instruction in the faith but culminating in theoria, a direct, intuitive vision of God. This trajectory mirrors the Greek understanding of initiation as a gradual unveiling, an ascent from shadows to light.

The imprint of Platonic thought is unmistakable here. The soul, as in Plato's philosophy, must transcend the realm of illusion and ascend toward the Divine. Yet Christianity recasts this ascent not as an intellectual exercise but as an intimate communion with a personal God.

HIDDENNESS AND REVELATION IN THE MYSTICAL PATH

This interplay of hiddenness and revelation did not vanish with the early Church but became a hallmark of Christian mysticism. The writings of later mystics, from Gregory of Nyssa to Pseudo-Dionysius the Areopagite, echo this paradox.

Gregory, deeply influenced by Greek thought, envisioned the spiritual journey as an unending ascent into the infinite mystery of God. No final point of arrival exists, for each revelation only deepens the awareness of Yahweh's boundless nature. This ever-deepening knowledge, an unknowing that surpasses knowing, became central to mystical thought.

Pseudo-Dionysius introduced the concept of apophatic theology, the notion that God, in His essence, lies beyond all human categories. To encounter the infinite, one must relinquish all images, all words, all concepts, entering a luminous darkness where God is known beyond knowing.

THE GREEK LEGACY IN CHRISTIAN MYSTICISM

The Greek heritage within Christian mysticism is deep and enduring. The language of mystery, of initiation and transformation, provided a way of articulating the soul's journey toward divine union. While Christianity redefined mystery in the light of Christ's revelation, it kept its experiential core, the recognition that true knowledge of God is not merely taught but lived in ecstasy.

Mysticism is not a doctrine but a process, not an abstract theology but an ancient path. It calls the seeker to close their eyes to the illusions of the world, to silence the restless chatter of the mind, and to step into the sacred unknown. This is the legacy of the Greek tradition: the recognition that a divine union is not simply a matter of revelation but of participation, a mystery ever unveiled, yet never exhausted.

The path is both one of knowing and of unknowing, of revelation and concealment, drawing the soul ever deeper into the inexhaustible mystery of God.

FREEDOM OF SPIRITUALITY

Christian mysticism represents a profound journey toward spiritual liberation, guided by divine vision. Christian mysticism eludes a singular definition, with interpretations ranging from a general inclination toward transcendent experiences to a stringent requirement of devout Christian practice as a prerequisite for true mystical engagement. This divergence centres on the significance of doctrine within the mystical path. Some approach Christian mysticism with a focus on personal spiritual experiences, placing less emphasis on doctrinal adherence. In contrast, others maintain that a genuine Christian mystical journey necessitates a firm commitment to established teachings.

Christian mysticism aligns with fundamental Christian doctrines yet embraces the individual's subjective experience as vital to the mystical life. Engaging in Christian mysticism involves a deep respect for doctrinal teachings alongside a trust in one's personal spiritual experiences. Navigating this balance can be challenging.

Historically, figures like Galileo faced opposition from religious authorities when scientific discoveries appeared to contradict biblical interpretations. Over time, it became evident that such conflicts often stemmed from a rigid adherence to dogma rather than an openness to deeper understanding. While mysticism differs from science, a similar tension exists: mystical insights may sometimes seem at odds with established religious teachings.

Scriptural references reflect this dynamic. Proverbs 29:18 states, "Where there is no prophecy, the people cast off restraint, but happy are those who keep the law," suggesting that divine revelation supports adherence to divine law. Conversely, Colossians 2:18–19 warns against being misled by those who, "insisting on self-abasement and worship of angels, dwelling on visions," become "puffed up without cause by a human way of thinking," indicating that pride in personal visions can lead away from true spiritual growth.

Resolving the paradox between doctrinal conformity and personal mystical experience requires discernment and guidance from wise spiritual mentors. This process is not about control but about maintaining the integrity of Christian mysticism. Recognising that not all spiritual insights align with Christian teachings is crucial. The most esteemed Christian mystics have demonstrated humility by seeking counsel to discern the congruence of their experiences with their faith. Relinquishing personal visions that conflict with foundational beliefs, though difficult, ultimately serves the greater good—the glorification of God and the well-being of the Christian community. However, it is important to note that mysticism challenges interpretations minimising mystical expositions and experiences to underpin dogmatic and religious approaches.

CHRIST AS THE CENTRE OF MYSTICAL CHRISTIANITY

Mysticism, though not confined to Christianity, reaches one of its most profound expressions in the person of Jesus Christ. The term mysticism is relatively modern, gaining prominence only in recent centuries. It was unknown to the great Christian contemplatives, yet the essence it conveys, an intimate and transformative encounter with Christ, has always been the heartbeat of Christian spirituality.

"The heart of mysticism is Jesus." — Ruth Burrows

To understand Christian mysticism, we must not only consider the broader nature of mysticism but also the distinctive way it manifests in Christ. This requires turning our gaze to Jesus of Nazareth, the Christós, the anointed one. Yet, encountering Jesus as a mystic is not without its difficulties, for across history, his image has been interpreted in many ways. The poet Gerard Manley Hopkins speaks of how "Christ plays in ten thousand places", an insight into the deeply personal yet universal nature of the encounter with him.

In order to understand Jesus as the ultimate mystic, it is important to distinguish the mystical aspects from the distortions that have obscured His true nature. Jesus has often been portrayed as a severe and judgmental figure rather than one of love and divine closeness. An example of this can be seen in the mosaic at the Basilica of the National Shrine of the Immaculate Conception in Washington, DC, where Christ appears with a stern and wrathful expression. This portrayal fails to capture the essence of His message, depicting Him more as a judge rather than the way into the mysteries of divinity. Such depictions can create misconceptions on the path to mysticism. When Jesus is perceived as distant or wrathful, the invitation to unite with Him may feel more like a burden than an opportunity. The true mystical vision of Christ, as reflected in the Gospels and the writings of Christian mystics, reveals a being of limitless mercy. He serves as the connection between the finite and the infinite, the doorway through which divine love and unity flow freely.

The Gospels clearly show instances of Jesus expressing anger, but it is never trivial or unkind. His anger is directed against injustice, hypocrisy, and exploitation, always in support of love and truth. However, intertwined with this righteous anger is a deep sense of compassion. Jesus not only confronts wrongdoing but also shows great tenderness by healing the sick, feeding the hungry, forgiving sinners, and welcoming the marginalised. These actions reveal a love that is revolutionary and inclusive, a love central to Christian mysticism a hunger and passion for restoration..

Jesus's teachings, as much as His actions, form the basis of the mystical path. While traditional Christianity has emphasised Jesus's actions - his miracles, crucifixion, and resurrection - their true significance is truly understood when viewed in light of his teachings. His perspective went beyond mere moral guidance; it was an insight into the interdependence of everything, a revelation of the divine essence intertwined within every aspect of life.

Mystics from various walks often discuss nonduality, which refers to the realisation that the apparent distinctions in life (such as light and dark, sacred and secular, self and other) are ultimately harmonised in a larger unity. In the Sermon on the Mount, He proclaims, "Love your enemies and pray for those who persecute you, so that you may be children of your Father in heaven. He causes his sun to rise on the evil and the good, and sends rain on the righteous and the unrighteous" (Matthew 5:44-45). This goes beyond mere ethical guidance; it reveals a deeper truth—an encouragement to perceive the world through God's eyes and to love as God does.

When Jesus says, "Be perfect, therefore, as your heavenly Father is perfect" (Matthew 5:48), he is not asking for a strict moral perfectionism but for a willingness to embrace completeness within us, a mystical entanglement. This all-encompassing acceptance is the mystical journey that breaks down the illusion of division and separation, guiding us to recognise the sacredness present in everything.

DIVINE UNION: THE HEART OF CHRISTIAN MYSTICISM

At the core of Christian mysticism lies the mystery of the divine union: Jesus's oneness with God, and our oneness with Him. The Gospel of John unveils this truth with striking clarity. Jesus proclaims, "I and the Father are one" (John 10:30) and later, "I am in my Father, and you are in me, and I am in you" (John 14:20). These words are not abstract theology; they are a living invitation into the very chambers of the heart of God.

Jesus prays, "that they may all be one, just as you, Father, are in me, and I in you, that they also may be in us" (John 17:21). This is the essence of Christian mysticism: a call to recognise and embody divine oneness. To live in this awareness is to see the world transfigured, to move through life with the certainty that the sacred is not distant but present in every moment, every encounter, and every living thing within creation.

The life, death, and resurrection of Jesus creates a mystical map of transformation. This mystery reveals that death is not the final destination but a gateway to new life. This pattern serves as the blueprint for the spiritual journey. Throughout life, we experience metaphorical deaths such as the end of relationships, the shedding of old identities, and the breaking of illusions. However, after these losses, resurrection is waiting. Christian mysticism emphasises that embracing these cycles of loss and renewal is the path to unlocking union with the divine. The cross is the portal to transfiguration. The empty tomb is not merely a historical event but the lived experience of those who move through the trials of life into the vastness of new life in Christ. Death has lost its sting, and for those embracing this mystery means walking in faith, understanding that every perceived ending holds a new beginning, one that's in the life of immortality. It is to live, as Paul described, "hidden with Christ in God" (Colossians 3:3), surrendered to the unfolding mystery of divine love.

Christian mysticism is centred around Jesus Christ. His life, teachings, and presence unveil the way to divine union, radical love, and transformation. To follow this ancient path, we need to let go of our misconceptions of Him and meet the Christ of the mystics - the One who looks at us with unwavering love, inviting us into the profound mysteries of divinity, unlocking gateways to divine connection and transformation, and revealing the beauty of primordial existence.

Jesus is not just a pointer to the truth, but He embodies the truth. He doesn't just talk about the way; He is The Way. For those who will embark on a journey with Him into the profound depths of His heart, He is not only the source of life but life itself. Embracing Him leads to awakening, seeing the world illuminated by the light of God's presence, entering a profound mystery where everything is united, and love is the ultimate ruler.

... allow the self to be unmade and remade in the quiet fire of divine love

Characteristics of a Mystic

THE MYSTIC IS ONE WHO SEEKS DIVINE UNION

Discipline: Contemplative Prayer & Meditation

Contemplative prayer is not merely an act of quietude; it is the sacred art of emptying, a surrender into the vast and boundless depths where the finite mind dissolves into the eternal mystery of God. It is the soul's pilgrimage beyond the veil of intellectualism, beyond the clamour of thought, into the formless expanse where Yahweh whispers in the language of silence.

To enter this state is to step into the Cloud of Unknowing,

that luminous darkness where the intellect can no longer grasp, and yet the heart begins to entangle. Here, God does not reveal Himself in the structure of words or the form of concepts, but in the infinite stillness, in the hush where the soul is drawn beyond itself. The mystic, emptied of selfhood, becomes a chalice, open, waiting, receptive to the influx of divine radiance.

This sacred practice requires an intentional withdrawal, a retreat not from the external world but from the turbulence of the inner dialogue. It is a descent into the silence beneath silence, the stillness beneath stillness, where the sacred presence hums like a secret chord woven into being. Through breath, through the sacred repetition of a single word, an invocation, a name, a prayer, consciousness is refined like gold, until all that remains is the luminous awareness of Yahweh. In mysticism, the prayer becomes the rhythm of the spirit, a ceaseless chant that harmonises the heart with the heartbeat of God. In Hitbodedut (self-secluded Jewish meditation), is the outpouring of the soul in solitude, the raw and intimate speaking to God, a conversation that unravels into union.

Some mystics enter this sacred space through vision, allowing divine light to permeate the soul, illuminating the hidden sanctuary within, where heaven and earth converge. Others find themselves drawn into the depths of the sacred darkness, where God is encountered not as an object of knowledge but as a Presence beyond presence, in which all things are known by unknowing.

Over time, this practice is no longer something the mystic does but something the mystic becomes. Prayer ceases to be an action and becomes a state of being. The veil between seen and unseen things, where the sacred pulse of the Infinite is felt within the marrow of existence. The mystic is no longer separate from the light but is immersed in it, carried by it, becoming a living song to Yahweh.

To engage in contemplative prayer is to surrender to the Great Mystery, to allow the self to be unmade and remade in the quiet fire of divine love. It is the crossing of a threshold into the eternal NOW, where nothing is sought, and yet all is found.

"Be still and know that I am God." (Psalm 46:10)

"No thought can grasp You at all." (Zohar)

"The secret of the Lord is with them that fear Him." (Psalm 25:14)

THE MYSTIC EMBODIES DIVINE WISDOM

Discipline: Sacred Study & Divine Contemplation

The mystic doesn't just read scripture; they drink of it as a sacred potion, drinking its essence as a living revelation. The holy words are not lifeless ink on paper, but currents of divine breath, whispering secrets to the soul. Through meditative immersion, the mystic moves beyond the realm of intellect into the luminous expanse of divine gnosis, a knowing that is not learned but unveiled. This is no mere study; it is an initiation, an encounter where the sacred text ceases to be an object and instead becomes a portal, a living voice calling from eternity.

This practice unfolds through a slow and reverent reading, where the words, like seeds, are planted deep within the heart to take root and blossom in their appointed time. In Jewish mysticism, this is embodied in Talmud Torah, where scripture is not just studied but contemplated, chanted, and turned over like a gem, catching the light of Elohim. The sacred reading known as lectio divina (monastic prayer and meditation) becomes a rhythmic ascent, reading, meditating, praying, and finally resting in wordless communion with God.

Mystics often invoke the power of sound, chanting the sacred words so that their vibrations echo within the soul, stirring remembrance of primordial existence in Him. Some trace the letters with their hands, writing and rewriting scripture as a sacred act of embodiment. Others take a single word or phrase and dwell upon it in silent rapture, waiting for its hidden fire to ignite within them. Through this deep and holy engagement, the mystic becomes a vessel of revelation, allowing divine wisdom to transfigure knowledge into enlightened experience, where the sacred is no longer read but becomes a living expression.

> "The fear of the Lord is the beginning of wisdom." (Proverbs 9:10)

> "By means of thirty-two wondrous paths of wisdom, Yah formed His creation." (Sefer Yetzirah 1:1)

> "Wisdom is poured out like water, and the glory of the Lord fills all the earth." (1 Enoch 49:1)

THE MYSTIC MASTERS THE SACRED NAMES

Discipline: Invocation of the Divine Names

Mystics across the ages have known that the Name of God is more than a spoken word. It is a key, a cypher unlocking the infinite. To invoke the Name is to summon the very essence of the Eternal, drawing the soul into harmony with the celestial currents that flow through creation. Chanting, meditating, or contemplating these sacred names is not an exercise; it is an act of divine synchronization, a way of aligning one's spirit with the ineffable mystery. Each name is a prism through which the Divine Light refracts, revealing different facets of the One beyond all names.

SACRED NAMES OF ELOHIM:

YHVH יהוה (Tetragrammaton) - The Name veiled in silence, resonating beyond sound and form. It is the breath of existence itself, the unspoken pulse of Being.

Elohim אֱלֹהִים - The Name of divine power and cosmic order, the force through which worlds are shaped, the balance of justice and mercy.

Ehyeh Asher Ehyeh אֶהְיֶה אֲשֶׁר אֶהְיֶה (I Am That I Am) - The self-revealing utterance from the Burning Bush, a proclamation of eternal presence, the unfolding mystery of the inexpressible.

Adonai אֲדֹנָי - The Name with reverence, a bridge between the ineffable and the spoken, the call of the devoted heart to the sovereign Lord.

El Shaddai אֵל שַׁדַּי - "God Almighty," the Name of boundless might and provision, the refuge of those who seek shelter beneath the wings of the Infinite.

Jesus/Yeshua יֵשׁוּעַ - In Christian mysticism, the Name above all names, the Word made flesh, a vessel of divine intercession, healing, and redemption. To invoke it is to draw near to the Heart of God.

72 Names of God are a mystical sequence of three-letter divine names derived from Exodus 14:19-21, a passage describing the splitting of the Red Sea. These names are used for spiritual ascension, meditation, and entangling the essence of Yahweh.

The 72 Names are formed from three consecutive verses in Exodus 14:19-21, each containing exactly 72 letters in the Hebrew text.

1. Exodus 14:19 — "And the angel of God, who had been travelling in front of Israel's camp, withdrew and went behind them..."

2. Exodus 14:20 — "It came between the camp of Egypt and the camp of Israel..."

3. Exodus 14:21 — "Then Moses stretched out his hand over the sea, and the LORD drove the sea back..."

The method of deriving the 72 Names is as follows:

- Step 1: Write the 72 letters of the first verse in order.

- Step 2: Write the 72 letters of the second verse backwards (in reverse order).

- Step 3: Write the 72 letters of the third verse in order again.

- Step 4: Combine these three rows vertically into 72 sets of three-letter sequences.

Each three-letter combination forms one of the 72 divine names.

To speak or chant these Names is to step beyond the veil, to let divine syllables shape realms, opening it to the sacred breath that gives life to all things. In the vibratory resonance of these holy utterances, the mystic does not merely call upon God, the mystic enters the Name and is drawn into the of each letter

PRACTICAL APPLICATIONS:

SACRED PRACTICES OF DIVINE ATTUNEMENT

To chant, to breathe, to inscribe, these are not acts but doorways into the Infinite. Through sacred repetition, the mystic does not simply speak the Divine Name but enters it, allowing the sacred syllables to vibrate through the soul, reshaping the self into a vessel of holy resonance. These ancient practices dissolve the illusion of separation, drawing the mystic into the radiant Presence that has no beginning and no end.

Chanting the Sacred Name - The rhythmic repetition of divine names is a path of immersion, a sacred current that carries the soul into deep communion. Mystics chant the permutations of YHVH יהוה, weaving the holy letters into breath and sound, while envisioning divine light flooding their being.

Breath as Invocation - The Name of God is the very breath of existence. To inhale with Yah יה and exhale with Weh וה is to surrender to the rhythm of creation itself. With each breath, the mystic dissolves further into the sacred flow, awakening to the divine breath that animates all life.

Vision of the Divine Letters - The Hebrew letters are not just symbols but living vessels of divine power. To contemplate them is to gaze into the fabric of creation. Some envision the letters of the Sacred Name glowing with celestial fire, others arrange them into sacred geometric forms, seeing in their interplay the hidden architecture of the universe. The mystic allows these visions to fill the body, illuminating every cell with divine radiance.

The Sacred Art of Inscription - The scribe is more than a writer; they are a channel through which divine energy flows. In the mystical traditions, scribes meditate upon the Names as they inscribe them, tracing each letter with reverence, invoking the holy properties they contain. Through this act, the written word becomes more than ink—it becomes an embodiment of divine presence.

Through these sacred practices, mystics attunes their consciousness to the immortal, dissolving the veils between human perception and divine reality. The Name ceases to be something spoken; it becomes experienced and expressed. The mystic no longer calls upon divinity from afar. They awaken to the truth that they have never been apart.

> "I have manifested Your Name unto the men which You gave me." (John 17:6)

> "He that calls on the Name of the Lord shall be delivered." (Joel 2:32)

THE MYSTIC WALKS BETWEEN WORLDS

Discipline: Prophetic Dreaming & Visionary States

Mystics transcend the limits of the physical world, becoming wanderers of the unseen and travelers between realms. Through sacred discipline and surrender, they venture beyond ordinary perception, entering luminous landscapes where divine revelations unfold. In dreams, trances, and raptures, they ascend, behold, and undergo transformation. These mystics serve as gateways to the infinite.

Prophetic Dreaming - The night holds a sacred significance as the boundary between worlds becomes faint. Mystics, such as Joseph and Daniel, are gifted with visions during sleep, their dreams intertwined with divine messages. Within these nighttime experiences, symbols blaze with concealed significance, directing the soul on its predetermined journey.

Trance and Ecstatic Rapture - By practising solitude and rhythmic breathing, the mystic calms the mind and unlocks the spirit, accessing altered states where the heavens reveal themselves. While the body stays grounded on earth, the spirit ascends in realms where the frequency of God echoes translating the body into trans-like states of ecstasy.

Ascension - is when mystics transcend the limitations of the physical body, rising into celestial realms. Enoch, during his ascension, was transported into heavenly dimensions, witnessing the structure of the celestial planes. These experiences expose the underlying structure of reality, uncovering enigmas too immense for ordinary consciousness to comprehend.

Merkavah Mysticism - involves engaging in deep contemplation, where they imagine themselves ascending on a chariot throne. They rise through the seven heavens, meeting celestial beings and basking in divine radiance centred around the Throne. It is a path taken by those yearning for the dimensional presence of Yahweh, their souls ablaze with longing for the revelation of the Throne Room of God.

Tongues and groaning - In the depths of divine ecstasy, language fades away into sacred frequencies. Words that are not of this world but of the spirit flow out, a language of pure connection beyond human speech, resonating with the uncreated light and vibrations of God.

PRACTICAL APPLICATIONS:

Guided Meditation: With eyes closed and spirit open, the mystic ascends the celestial stairway, climbing Jacob's ladder (DNA staircase) into the realms of light. Some traverse the heavenly spheres, guided by the radiance of divine messengers, ascending higher into the Infinite.

Lucid Dreaming - The realm of dreams is a sacred dimension where mystery whispers. By setting an intention before sleep and keeping a dream journal, the mystic prepares to receive revelations in the silent hours, walking the path of vision during sleep.

Breath Control & Sacred Chanting - The breath is more than just air; it is the rhythm of divine life. Combining rhythmic breathing with chanting sacred names allows the mystic to reach an elevated state where visions emerge. With each inhale, the Presence is embraced; with each exhale, obstacles to progress are released.

Sacred Anointing & Incense - The fragrance of the sacred lingers in the air, opening the heart to the unseen. Essential oils spiral heavenward, positioned as a bridge between realms. Oils are placed upon the body and face, aligning the senses with frequency and fragrance, preparing them for divine reception.

"I beheld the heavens opened." (Ezekiel 1:1)

THE MYSTIC'S VISION OF COSMIC ONENESS

Sacred Attunement: Awakening to Gods Divine Presence in All Things

For mystics, the universe transcends a collection of forms; it's a radiant, living whole, divinely woven. Each breath, movement, and tree whisper holds the secret rhythm of the Infinite, reflecting the Eternal speaking itself into existence. The awakened soul perceives the world as a manifestation of divine unity, a resonant field of sacred interconnection where the illusion of separation dissolves into the One.

In this sacred vision, the mystic moves beyond fragmented perception and beholds existence as a seamless expression of divine love. The veil of ordinary perception lifts, revealing the ever-present Shekinah, the indwelling Divine Presence spread over all creation. To perceive deeply is to behold the divine in everything, acknowledging the radiant essence of God in every aspect of existence.

MYSTICAL PATHWAYS TO UNITY

Shekinah's Embrace: The Divine Feminine indwells all that is, her presence shimmering in the leaves, the stars, and the spaces between words.

Sacramental Vision: Every moment, every encounter, every act of being is charged with divine significance, a revelation awaiting recognition.

Interwoven Souls: The mystic sees all beings as reflections of Yahweh, interconnected sparks of a singular holy fire woven together in divine arcing.

Creation as Scripture: The natural world becomes a sacred text, each tree and river a letter in the unfolding revelation of God, as spoken of in the Psalms.

Sacred Geometry: The mathematics of creation—fractals, spirals, Fibonacci patterns—whisper the symmetry of divine intelligence, shaping the very structure of existence.

Divine Resonance: Experience the sacred—not just visually but aurally and sensorial, through sacred chants, resonant mantras, and vibrational harmonics that harmonise soul and cosmos.

> "In Him we live, and move, and have our being." (Acts 17:28)
>
> "The whole earth is full of His glory." (Isaiah 6:3)
>
> "For the earth will be filled with the knowledge of the glory of the Lord as the waters cover the sea." (Habakkuk 2:14)
>
> "The heavens declare the glory of God; the skies proclaim the work of His hands." (Psalm 19:1)
>
> "Enoch walked with God, and he was not, for God took him." (Genesis 5:24)

In the profound domain of sacred perception, the mystic doesn't simply believe in unity, they embody it. The lines between self and the universe fade away, leading to the understanding that they were never truly apart. Seeing with clarity means recognising the presence of God in all things. Therefore, the mystic transcends the illusionary barrier and enters the luminous realm of unity, oneness, where everything reveals the eternal truth: God, Elohim, Yahweh, Yeshua, Holy Spirit is the only reality.

THE MYSTIC SPEAKS IN SYMBOLS & PARADOXES

Discipline: Sacred Symbolism & Allegorical Interpretation

Truths too profound for words are clothed in parables, visions, and mysteries. The use of symbolism allows the mystic to communicate divine insights that transcend literal expression, ensuring that deeper meanings are revealed only to those prepared to receive them.

Mystics frequently interpret sacred texts allegorically, understanding their deeper meanings beyond the surface. In Jewish Midrashic tradition, biblical narratives are viewed as containing multiple layers of meaning, from the literal to the mystical. Similarly, Christian mystics like Meister Eckhart and St. John of the Cross employed poetic and paradoxical language to describe their experiences of Christ.

Paradox also plays a crucial role in mystical teaching, where seemingly contradictory statements—such as "To find yourself, you must lose yourself"—act as gateways to higher understanding. This method forces the mind to move beyond conventional logic and embrace divine wisdom.

"To you it is given to know the mysteries of the kingdom." (Luke 8:10)

"These are the hidden things revealed." (Zohar)

"The wise shall understand." (Daniel 12:10)

... humans
are a micro
representation of
the divine dwelling

The mysticism of Moses and Paul

THE APOSTLE PAUL: THE QUINTESSENTIAL MYSTIC OF THE NEW TESTAMENT

The Apostle Paul is considered the quintessential mystic of the New Testament. His life, writings, and teachings show a profound engagement with divine mysteries and spiritual experiences. While people primarily celebrate Paul as a theologian, evangelist, and church planter, his mystical dimensions offer a deeper lens through which to understand his contributions to Christian thought. This exploration will examine Paul's history as a mystic, the reasons for establishing him the quintessential New Testament mystic, his use of mystical language, key scriptures focused on mysticism, and references to his mystical nature in other writings.

PAUL'S HISTORY AS A MYSTIC

Paul's mystical journey began dramatically on the road to Damascus, as recorded in Acts 9:1–9. This transformative encounter with the risen Christ, a vision so intense that it temporarily blinded him, became the cornerstone of his spiritual life and mission. This experience was not merely a conversion; it was an initiation into the mysteries of Christ. Paul himself described this event as a divine unveiling (Galatians 1:12), emphasising that his gospel came "not from man, but through a revelation of Jesus Christ." This emphasis on direct, revelatory knowledge through experiential downloads characterises the mystic's path.

Many mystical experiences marked Paul's life. In 2 Corinthians 12:2–4, he recounts being "caught up to the third heaven," where he heard "inexpressible things" that human words could not convey.

"I know a man in Christ who fourteen years ago was caught up to the third heaven. Whether it was in the body or out of the body, I do not know, God knows. And I know that this man, whether in the body or apart from the body I do not know, but God knows, was caught up to paradise and heard inexpressible things, things that no one is permitted to tell." 2 Corinthians 12:2-4 NIV.

This event underscores his intimate participation in heavenly realities and his deep communion with God. Such experiences set Paul apart as a mystic who not only contemplated divine mysteries but also took part in them. It's a key aspect of the mystical lifestyle, knowing Jesus and everything else that exists in and through Him… EVERYTHING!

WHY IS PAUL CONSIDERED THE QUINTESSENTIAL NEW TESTAMENT MYSTIC?

Paul's mysticism is foundational to his theology and his vision of a Christian mystical life. Unlike others, Paul articulates a systematic understanding of union with Christ, a central theme in Christian mysticism. His frequent use of phrases like "in Christ" or "Christ in me" reflects a process of inner transformation that transcends moral or intellectual adherence. For Paul, to be a believer meant mystical union with Christ, sharing in His death, resurrection, and glorification (Galatians 2:20)

Moreover, Paul's mysticism is communal as well as individual. His epistles emphasise the Ekklesia as the "Body of Christ" (1 Corinthians 12:27) and describe believers as collectively taking part in the mystery of God's redemptive plan. This vision of mystical union extends beyond personal enlightenment to encompass the entire cosmos, which Paul sees as being reconciled to God through Christ (Colossians 1:19–20). The entire cosmos, what a glorious participation.

Paul also bridges Jewish mystical ways with the emerging Christian faith. His background as a Pharisee, deeply steeped in the Hebrew Scriptures, equipped him to reinterpret Jewish mystical motifs, such as the heavenly ascent, divine glory, and the hidden wisdom of God in the light of Christ. This synthesis makes Paul not only a mystic but also a theologian of mystical integration.

> It's quite simple actually, a mystics journey is that of unlocking the divine union we have in Him. To see it materialise in pure ecstasy through living a life enraptured by His beauty and challenging the limitations imposed by religious traditions.

PAUL'S USE OF THE WORD 'MYSTIC' IN HIS WRITINGS

While Paul never explicitly uses the Greek word 'mystikos' (μυστικός), he frequently employs the related term 'mystērion' (μυστήριον), which translates to "mystery." This term appears approximately 21 times in his letters, more than any other New Testament author. For Paul, the "mystery" is not something inaccessible but a divine truth once hidden and now revealed in Christ (Ephesians 3:3–5; Colossians 1:26–27).

"the mystery that has been kept hidden for ages and generations but is now disclosed to the Lord's people. To them God has chosen to make known among the Gentiles the glorious riches of this mystery, which is Christ in you, the hope of glory." Colossians 1:26-27 NIV.

Paul's use of 'mysterion' often conveys a deeply mystical understanding of God's plan for humanity. For example, in 1 Corinthians 2:7, he speaks of "God's wisdom, a mystery hidden and that God destined for our glory before time began." This reflects the mystic's preoccupation with unveiling divine realities that transcend human comprehension.

KEY SCRIPTURES FROM PAUL CENTRED AROUND MYSTICISM

Paul's writings are filled with passages that resonate with mystical themes. Some of the most significant include:

1. Romans 8:9–11: Paul speaks of the indwelling Spirit as the presence of God within believers, a core mystical idea of divine union.

2. Galatians 2:20: "I have been crucified with Christ and I no longer live, but Christ lives in me." This verse encapsulates Paul's mystical theology of self-transcendence and union with Christ. Religion so easily misinterprets the scripture that you are nothing and God is everything. Jesus' everythingness is not dependent on your nothingness. The divine union encompasses the mystical entanglement of our primordial existence in Him, a memory that binds us together. To Him, we are everything; you wouldn't be here if you were insignificant.

3. 1 Corinthians 2:6–16: Paul contrasts human wisdom with the spiritual wisdom revealed by the Spirit, emphasising the mystic's access to divine knowledge. Read the book by my friend Justin Paul Abraham 'BEYOND HUMAN'.

4. 2 Corinthians 12:2–4: Paul's vision of the "third heaven" underscores his direct experience of divine realities beyond

the physical realm. I love this one. Being enraptured into the heavenly realms, we can commune with our spiritual family, i.e. the cloud of witnesses and the angelic realms.

5. Colossians 1:26–27: Paul describes the mystery hidden for ages but now revealed, which is "Christ in you, the hope of glory." This is the ultimate high. The entanglement of 'as He is, so are we' in this reality. The ecstasy of the mirror image of Christ revealed in us.

6. Ephesians 3:14–19: Paul prays for believers to "know the love of Christ that surpasses knowledge," a quintessential mystical aspiration. The wine house of the love of Jesus. It's the pub of his love. Once you start drinking there, you ain't ever getting out sober again. Who would want to, anyhow?

OTHER WRITINGS THAT MENTION PAUL AS A MYSTIC

Theologians, mystics, and scholars have widely acknowledged Paul's mystical dimensions throughout history. Early Church Fathers, such as Origen and Augustine, viewed Paul as a mystic whose writings revealed profound spiritual insights. Augustine, for instance, frequently referenced Paul's concept of "Christ in us" to articulate his own mystical theology.

In the Middle Ages, Paul's writings inspired Christian mystics like Bernard of Clairvaux, Meister Eckhart, and Julian of Norwich. They often drew on Paul's descriptions of union with Christ and the indwelling Spirit to articulate their mystical experiences. Bernard, for example, saw Paul's vision of the "third heaven" as a model for the soul's ascent to God.

Modern scholarship also highlights Paul's mysticism. Scholars such as Albert Schweitzer, E.P. Sanders, and N.T. Wright has emphasised the mystical elements in Paul's theology, particularly his understanding of participation in Christ. Schweitzer's seminal work, *The Mysticism of Paul the Apostle*, argues that Paul's central theological concept is a mystical union with Christ, which shapes every aspect of his thought.

His influence extends beyond Christianity. Jewish mystical traditions, particularly Kabbalistic interpretations, portray Paul as someone bridging Jewish and Christian mysticism. Though these interpretations remain speculative, they underscore the cross-cultural and inter-religious significance of Paul's mystical legacy.

The Apostle Paul stands as the quintessential mystic of the New Testament because of his profound engagement with divine mysteries and his transformative spiritual experiences. His mystical theology, centred on union with Christ, offers a vision of Christian life that is both deeply personal and universally inclusive. Through his frequent use of 'mystērion' and his emphasis on the hidden wisdom of God, Paul invites believers into a mystical relationship with the divine transcending religious boundaries.

Paul's writings, filled with references to heavenly visions, spiritual wisdom, and the indwelling presence of Christ, have inspired countless mystics throughout history. His legacy as a mystic continues to shape Christian spirituality, offering a path of divine intimacy and transcendent hope for generations to come.

MOSES: THE QUINTESSENTIAL MYSTIC OF THE OLD TESTAMENT

His life, experiences, and writings embody the essence of Old Testament mysticism. Moses' encounters with God reveal an unparalleled intimacy and direct communion with Yahweh, marking him as a central figure in Jewish and Christian mystical traditions. Therefore, Moses is considered the quintessential mystic:

From his encounter with the burning bush (Exodus 3:1–12) to his final moments on Mount Nebo (Deuteronomy 34:1–5), Moses lived a life filled with mystical experiences. These encounters had a profound impact not only on Moses himself but also on the Israelites, as he played the role of mediator between God and His people. What distinguishes Moses is that his experiences were not limited to visions and dreams; he actually experienced them in tangible form. Moses underwent physical ascensions and encounters, engaging with the spiritual realm holistically, involving his spirit, soul, and body.

The Burning Bush: Moses' first direct encounter with God occurs in an extraordinary physical vision of a bush that burns without being consumed. This event is mystical in nature, as Moses enters sacred ground and hears the divine voice of God calling him on a prophetic mission of redemption.

Mount Sinai and the Giving of the Law: The summit of Moses' mysticism is his ascent of Mount Sinai, where he speaks with God "face to face" (Exodus 33:11). This moment signifies an unparalleled intimacy and the reception of divine revelation that shaped Israel's covenantal identity.

The Glory of God: In Exodus 34:29–35, Moses descends from Sinai with his face shining, reflecting the glory of God. This physical manifestation of divine presence marks Moses as one who has entered a mystical union with the transcendent presence of God.

WHY MOSES IS THE QUINTESSENTIAL MYSTIC OF THE OLD TESTAMENT

Moses' mystical experiences form the foundation of the Jewish understanding of divine encounter and covenantal theology. Key reasons for his prominence include:

Direct Encounter with God: Moses is described as speaking with God "face to face, as one speaks to a friend" (Exodus 33:11). This level of intimacy with Yahweh is unmatched in the Old Testament. You might wonder, what sets apart the mystical encounter with God from that of all Christians? Well, for a mystic, as depicted in the Hebrew account of Moses' encounter, it goes beyond a mere face-to-face experience. It delves into a profound face INTO face encounter. It's not solely about the external interaction but rather the profound depths within the face itself. It involves becoming intertwined with the very breath of Yahweh and ascending into the realms contained within that breath.

The role of Moses as a mediator between God and His people: He serves as a bridge, conveying divine laws and instructions. This position embodies a mystic, translating divine secrets into human comprehension. A mystic embraces their identity as a Hebrew עבר, which translates to 'to cross over' - they act as a bridge, bringing the mystical into the physical realm. Similarly, in Christ, you serve as the cosmic gate, connecting different realms and dimensions, enabling manifestation here on earth.

Visible Manifestation and Transformation: His encounters with God bring about profound change, not just within himself but also within the entire community. This inner transformation of the interior castle is then reflected in outward manifestation and restoration.

USE OF MYSTICAL LANGUAGE IN THE WRITINGS ATTRIBUTED TO MOSES

The Pentateuch, which comprises the first five books in the Bible, has traditionally been attributed to Moses. Within its pages, we find an abundance of mystical themes and references. Although the term "mystic" is not explicitly used, the text is replete with depictions of divine mysteries, concealed wisdom, and sacred encounters.

The Name of God: In Exodus 3:14, Moses is given the divine name of God, "I AM WHO I AM" (Ehyeh-Asher-Ehyeh). This revelation of God's ineffable nature is profoundly mystical, reflecting a God beyond human comprehension. Traditional Christianity contains God, mystics aim to encounter and express the incomprehensible, the beyond human experience.

The Tabernacle, as described in Exodus 25–31, provides detailed instructions that unveil the profound concept of sacred space as a dwelling for God's presence among His people. Through the Tabernacle, Moses had the privilege of glimpsing the temple and understanding the mystical truth that humans are a micro representation of the divine dwelling. We are intricately connected as the temple of Yahweh, embodying both its pattern and mirror image.

Hidden Wisdom and revelation: According to Deuteronomy

29:29, it is stated that "The secret things belong to the Lord our God, but the things revealed belong to us." This recognition of divine mystery is in line with the mystical journey of uncovering hidden and revealed secrets. Mystics embark on a quest for treasure, seeking the profound aspects of God that transcend conventional boundaries, immersing themselves in a thrilling journey of experiencing and discovering the kingdom of God and its spiritual foundations.

KEY SCRIPTURES CENTRED AROUND MYSTICISM

Several passages in the Pentateuch highlight Moses' mystical nature:

1. Exodus 3:1–6: The burning bush encounter, symbolising divine revelation.

2. Exodus 19:16–20: The Sinai theophany, where Moses ascends into God's presence amidst fire, smoke, and thunder.

3. Exodus 33:18–23: Moses asks to see God's glory, receiving a revelation of God's presence and goodness.

4. Exodus 34:29–35: The shining face of Moses after speaking with God reflects divine transformation.

5. Numbers 12:6–8: God affirms Moses' unique prophetic role, speaking to him "clearly and not in riddles."

OTHER WRITINGS THAT MENTION MOSES AS A MYSTIC

Moses' mystical nature is acknowledged and explored in several later Jewish, Christian, and even Islamic writings:

JEWISH MYSTICISM:

The Zohar, a foundational text of mysticism, often reflects on Moses as a pattern of a mystic who ascends to divine realms and receives secret knowledge. The Midrash (ancient commentary of

Hebrew scriptures) elaborates on Moses' encounters with God, emphasising his unparalleled closeness to the Divine.

EARLY CHRISTIAN WRITINGS:

In the New Testament, Moses' mystical experiences are referenced to highlight the superiority of Christ (Hebrews 3:1–6) while affirming Moses' role as a mediator of divine revelation (2 Corinthians 3:7–18). The Transfiguration of Jesus (Matthew 17:1–8) includes Moses, symbolising his enduring significance in mystical theology.

MEDIEVAL MYSTICS:

In Gregory of Nyssa's 'Life of Moses', the life of Moses is interpreted as a symbolic representation of the soul's journey towards God. The emphasis lies on the mystical aspect of this journey, as the soul seeks to connect with the "invisible and infinite God." Similarly, Pseudo-Dionysius the Areopagite refers to Moses in his work 'Mystical Theology', specifically highlighting Moses' ascent into the mysterious "cloud of unknowing" on Mount Sinai.

ISLAMIC MYSTICISM:

In the Sufi tradition, Moses (Musa) is revered as both a mystic and a prophet who had direct encounters with Allah. These encounters are mentioned in the Qur'an, specifically in Surah 20:9–24. While our mysticism is firmly centred on Christ, we possess the wisdom and maturity to acknowledge and quote from non-Christian texts that align with biblical principles and references.

MOSES' LEGACY AS A MYSTIC

The mystical legacy of Moses continues to reverberate across various religious traditions, as his divine encounters serve as the quintessential example of a mystic who ventures into the presence of divinity. Through these encounters, he receives concealed wisdom and acts as a mediator, translating sacred mysticism to the community. Throughout history, both his life and writings have served as a profound source of inspiration for mystics from a range of backgrounds, including Jewish Kabbalists, Christian contemplatives, Islamic Sufis and other non-Christian writings. Moses' narrative teaches us that the mystical journey not only leads to personal transformation but also plays a vital role in bringing divine enlightenment into your immediate environment. As a prominent figure in the realm of mysticism, Moses stands tall as the archetypal mystic of the Old Testament.

... a deeper engagement with divine reality, transcending intellectual understanding and religious routine

The Transformative Power of Mystical Practice in Creation

The mystical path offers more than theoretical understanding or religious observance. It promises a profound transformation of consciousness. The apostles described this transformation as taking on "the mind of Christ" and taking part in His "divine nature."

This transformative journey occurs through integrating Christian wisdom with contemplative practice. It creates an alchemical process that can fundamentally reshape our way of being in the world. Moreover, this process affects every aspect of life, including our relationships, work, understanding of purpose, and approach to life challenges.

But that's not where it stops. For the mystic, every aspect of life that contains life has a divine purpose and blueprint for engagement. Take the scripture in Romans 8:19-22 (NIV):

"For the creation waits in eager expectation for the sons of God to be revealed. For the creation was subjected to frustration, not by its own choice, but by the will of the one who subjected it, in hope that the creation itself will be liberated from its bondage to decay and brought into the freedom and glory of the sons of God. We know that the whole creation has been groaning as in the pains of childbirth right up to the present time."

Creation itself has a purpose, and that purpose is closely entangled with mankind. If the sons of God start to walk in their divine purpose, authority and position in Christ, governing creation, the world around us is quickened into their original intent. Consider these examples from the early medieval mystics:

ST FRANCIS OF ASSISI

Paraphrased from the 'Canticle of the Sun': Under the Umbrian sun, Francis would walk the dusty paths between Assisi's olive groves with bare feet pressing his toes into the ground of the earth. Birds would gather around him, not in the cautious way they approach most humans, but settling on his shoulders and arms as if they were recognising a kindred spirit. When Francis opened his mouth to speak, he addressed them as "my little sisters, the birds," and they would fall silent, tilting their heads to listen. One famous encounter occurred near Bevagna, where Francis came upon a flock of birds of various species gathered in a field. Instead of scattering at his approach, they remained, prompting him to rush over with extraordinary joy. He spoke to them with passionate tenderness: "My sister birds, you owe much to God your Creator, and always and everywhere must praise Him." The birds would stretch their necks, extend their wings, and open their beaks in response to his words.

But perhaps his most profound encounter was with the wolf of

Gubbio. From 'The Wolf of Gubbio' Chapter XXI of the Fioretti: The townspeople lived in terror of this fierce creature until Francis went out to meet it. Upon finding the wolf, Francis didn't see a monster but a hungry, desperate creature of God. "Brother Wolf," he said, making the sign of the cross, "you do much harm in these parts." The wolf, which had been charging at Francis, slowed and then laid down at his feet like a lamb. Francis struck a pact between the wolf and the townspeople, they would feed the creature, and it would harm no one else. The wolf placed its paw in Francis's hand as a pledge, and for two years until its death, it walked peacefully through Gubbio's streets, a living testament to Francis's understanding that all creation exists within God's love.

HILDEGARD OF BINGEN

In the verdant Rhineland valley, Hildegard would wake before dawn to walk through the monastery's herb garden. Here, among the swaying plants wet with dew, she experienced what she called "viriditas", the sacred greening power of God. She saw in every leaf and stem not just physical matter but the living breath of divinity.

Hildegard wrote of her visions where the natural world revealed its secrets to her. She described how each plant whispered its healing purpose: sage spoke of its power to clarify the mind, fennel revealed its ability to bring joy, while roses taught her about the heart's mysteries. In her text "Physica," she recorded these conversations with creation, describing how God's love flowed through every natural thing.

One particular morning, as recorded in her writings, she sat beneath a great oak tree and experienced what she called "the shadow of Living Light." The tree's branches seemed to pulse with divine energy, and she suddenly understood how every created thing was connected in a vast web of life. She wrote: "The earth sweats germinating power from its very pores... The soul is the greening life force of the flesh, for it is the substance of God."

KEVIN OF GLENDALOUGH

From 'The medieval Irish Lives of the Saints': In the misty valleys of sixth-century Ireland, Kevin found his sanctuary in the wilderness of Glendalough. The ancient stories tell of how he would stand in the lake's cold waters at dawn, arms outstretched in prayer, so still and so long that birds mistook him for a branch. One blackbird in particular made its presence known, landing on his palm and beginning to build its nest.

For days, Kevin remained in prayer, his arm unwavering. The blackbird laid her eggs, and still Kevin stood, feeling the delicate weight of new life in his hand. Rain fell, wind blew, but he remained steady as an oak. When the eggs hatched, tiny beaks opened in his palm, and Kevin felt each heartbeat as if it were his own. He waited until the fledglings took wing before finally lowering his arm, understanding that his prayer had become not just words but a living act of communion with creation.

Other animals sought him out, too. An otter would bring him salmon from the lake each morning, laying the fish at his feet before disappearing back into the waters. Wild boars would grow calm in his presence, and deer would eat from his hand. The ancient Irish texts speak of how he could call forth a rowan tree to bear fruit out of season when someone was hungry, suggesting a deep connection not just with animals but with the plant world as well.

The modern Christian tendency to separate spiritual experiences into dispensationalism is problematic because modern culture lacks the medieval experiences that once contributed to the mystery described in Romans 8:19. As a result, the mystical is diminished for Christians. Ultimately, the mystical path teaches us to recognise and respond to the sacred dimension in everyday experiences in creation.

The mystical path not only helps us engage with concepts in ways that heal rather than harm but also encourages unity with all of creation instead of division. The mystic believes that part of the way is to bring restoration and healing to creation. Mysticism provides us with tools for personal transformation, while simultaneously fostering compassion and understanding in transforming creation. This approach is especially valuable in our diverse and interconnected world, where countless people are in search of spiritual depth without rigid dogmatism.

Christian mysticism invites you into a deeper engagement with divine reality, transcending intellectual understanding and religious routine. It challenges you to open yourself to transformation into authenticity. This journey creates openness, courage, and a willingness to explore scripture from dimensional perspectives and deeper realms, offering abundant resources for spiritual growth. It provides practical guidance for experiencing ascension realms of divine presence while meaningfully engaging with the world around you.

... a transformative doorway into a life marked by intimacy with Jesus

The Ecstasy of Mysticism

Mysticism, with its diverse expressions, embodies a profound and personal connection with Yahweh and His kingdom. This term encompasses a wide spectrum of experiences, states of consciousness, abilities, attitudes, and internal aspects of being a son of God and the process of becoming. By comprehending these different dimensions, you can better recognise the various ways in which mysticism manifests within Christianity.

THE MYSTICAL EXPERIENCE IN ECSTASY

The term ecstasy is derived from the Greek word ἔκστασις (ekstasis), which means "standing outside oneself" (ἔκ: "out of," στάσις: "standing"). In Greek culture, this state represents a profound experience of being enraptured, trance, or mysticism, where one loses their normal state of consciousness. Similar concepts can be found in Hebrew phrases, such as "נָפַל עָלָיו רוּחַ יְהֹוָה" (the Spirit of the LORD came upon him), which refers to prophetic inspiration or divine revelation, an infusion of a state that operates beyond human. Ecstasy symbolises a heightened spiritual or emotional awareness, often accompanied by visions or overwhelming joy. In both traditions, it denotes a transcendent state beyond ordinary perception or mental faculties.

Modern-day experiences of ecstasy involve spiritual moments when the indwelling Spirit is revealed. Mystical experiences occur during deep meditation, nature-induced awe, or experiences where individuals feel detached from reality. Creative flow states allow artists, writers, and musicians to lose themselves in their work. Psychedelic experiences from an intimate relationship with Jesus that creates altered perceptions and transcendence, being enraptured into the wine house of God. Emotional ecstasy also occurs in moments of overwhelming joy or love. All these experiences reflect a state of being outside ordinary consciousness.

The focus of mysticism is on spirituality in Christ, which sparks an overwhelming and indescribable experience known as ecstasy. During these moments, the soul appears to surpass the limits of the physical senses and glimpse the divine realms. These experiences go beyond mere emotional peaks; they reveal deeper spiritual truths that exist beyond what ordinary perception can grasp. Not only do these ecstatic encounters offer transformative insight into unseen dimensions, but they also serve as gateways to profound connections and entanglements with God. This form of ecstasy is genuine, not influenced by external factors or substances, but a revelation and encounter with the indwelling Spirit of God. Both biblical and extra-biblical texts vividly depict this divine ecstasy, confirming that it has played a central role in the spiritual journeys of countless mystics throughout history.

BIBLICAL EXAMPLES OF ECSTATIC ENCOUNTERS

The Transfiguration of Christ, described in Matthew 17:1-8, Mark 9:2-8, and Luke 9:28-36, is one of the most remarkable instances of divine ecstasy in the scriptures. Accompanied by Peter, James, and John, Jesus ascends a mountain, unveiling His divine nature in a brilliant display of light. His face radiates like the sun, and His garments take on a pristine whiteness of light itself (Matthew 17:2). In this awe-inspiring moment, Moses and Elijah appear, leaving the disciples in a state of both terror and wonder. Trying to comprehend this overwhelming experience, Peter suggests constructing tabernacles, longing to preserve the encounter. Their struggle to grasp the significance of this transcendent vision of Jesus's glorified state surpasses their ordinary understanding. Through this revelatory experience, they glimpse divine reality and bear witness to a multitude of cloud of witnesses.

The Conversion of Paul (Acts 9:1-19) tells the story of Saul, a zealous persecutor of Christians, encountering the risen Christ in a moment of blinding ecstasy on the road to Damascus. "Suddenly a light from heaven flashed around him. He fell to the ground and heard a voice say to him, 'Saul, Saul, why do you persecute me?'" (Acts 9:3-4). This ecstatic encounter leaves Paul physically blinded, symbolising a shattering of his previous perceptions. His inward eyes are opened to a new reality, saturated with the presence and bliss of Jesus. This transformative vision propels Paul into a life of apostolic mission and mystical intimacy with God, as seen in his later writings: "I have been crucified with Christ and I no longer live, but Christ lives in me" (Galatians 2:20).

The Vision of Isaiah (Isaiah 6:1-7) marks the prophet Isaiah's calling through an overwhelming vision of God's glory in the heavenly temple. "I saw the Lord, high and exalted, seated on a throne... Above him were seraphim... And they were calling to one another: 'Holy, holy, holy is the Lord Almighty; the whole earth is full of his glory'" (Isaiah 6:1-3). Isaiah's experience is so intense that he becomes acutely aware of his unworthiness, crying out: "Woe to me! I am ruined!" Yet this ecstatic encounter not only humbles him but also purifies and empowers him to fulfil his prophetic mission.

EXTRA-BIBLICAL SOURCES AND MYSTICAL TESTIMONIES

1. The Visions of Saint Teresa of Ávila

Saint Teresa, a Carmelite nun and mystic, describes her ecstatic encounters with God in *The Interior Castle*. She writes of moments where she feels lifted out of herself, experiencing a profound union with Yahweh:

"The soul feels such a delight that it would wish never to lose it... God implants Himself deeply in the interior of the soul."

In one famous vision, she recounts an angel piercing her heart with a golden spear, a metaphor for the ecstatic pain of divine love. This moment, she claims, leaves her soul burning with an indescribable passion for God.

2. Saint John of the Cross and the Dark Night of the Soul

In his writings, Saint John of the Cross explores the paradox of divine ecstasy that emerges even through spiritual darkness. In his mystical poem, *The Dark Night*, he describes how the soul, through purgative trials, is prepared to experience profound union with God:

"Oh, night that guided me,
Oh, night more lovely than the dawn,
Oh, night that joined Beloved with lover,
Lover transformed in the Beloved!"

This ecstatic experience of union with God, while veiled in darkness and suffering, reveals a reality more intimate and transcendent than human language can fully express.

3. The Jewish Mystical Tradition (Kabbalah)

In Jewish mysticism, particularly the Kabbalistic tradition, the concept of *Devekut* (clinging to God) reflects a form of ecstatic union. The *Zohar*, speaks of the soul ascending through layers of divine reality until it reaches an intimate encounter with the *Ein Sof* (the Infinite). These ascents are often accompanied by visions, feelings of burning love, and a dissolution of the self in God's presence.

THE TRANSFORMATIVE POWER OF ECSTASY

These mystical experiences of ecstasy can leave a permanent imprint on the soul. They function as:

- **Invitations to Deeper Communion**: Just as the Transfiguration drew Peter, James, and John into a greater understanding of Jesus' divine nature, moments of ecstasy invite the soul to pursue deeper intimacy with God beyond traditional recipes and formulas.

- **Catalysts for Spiritual Growth and Purpose**: Saint Paul's conversion demonstrates how divine ecstasy can radically change one's life direction, aligning the soul with divine purpose. Another example is 'The Toronto Blessing'. After an ecstatic experience of the love of the Farther ignited one of the greatest revival movements.

- **Foretastes of Eternal Union and Transformation**: These sparks of ecstasy create moments as described in Revelation, where, once experienced, leaves an undeniable mark of transformation. *"They will see His face, and His name will be on their foreheads"* (Revelation 22:4).

Mystical ecstasy is not an end in itself but a transformative doorway into a life marked by intimacy with Jesus. It transcends doctrine and tradition, drawing the soul into an experiential knowledge of God's infinite presence and love. Whether through a blinding vision, a moment of sublime light, or an ineffable sense of unity, these encounters resonate as divine invitations to abide in the boundless mystery of Yahweh.

... the essence of self-awareness of one's own existence, thoughts and surroundings

Mysticism as an Elevated State of Consciousness

One word that you will find is constantly spoken of is 'consciousness'. Beyond momentary experiences, mysticism can also describe a sustained shift in consciousness. This elevated awareness, sometimes called "enlightenment", transcends ordinary perception and aligns your mind and heart with the Divine rhythms of God's heart. In the words of Saint Paul, this involves allowing "the same mind to be in you that was in Christ Jesus" (Philippians 2:5). Unlike the fleeting nature of an epiphany, this state reflects an ongoing transformation of the self, an unlocking. This heightened consciousness manifests as an abiding sense of unity with God, a realisation that the boundaries separating self, others, and the Divine are ultimately based on illusion. It is the awareness that one's life is enveloped in divine grace. The great Christian mystics often spoke of this state as a form of spiritual marriage or union with God. For instance, the writings of Saint Teresa of Ávila describe the "interior castle" where the soul journeys toward deeper intimacy with God. Mystical consciousness is less about extraordinary visions and more about a consistent, holistic awareness of God's presence permeating all of life. Let's examine this in detail, as it plays a significant role in the life of a mystic.

WHAT IS CONSCIOUSNESS

Consciousness in its most basic form can be understood as the essence of self-awareness of one's own existence, thoughts and surroundings. It is the lens through which reality is perceived, a divine spark that entangles you to the Creator. Grounding this in Christian mysticism, alongside insights from quantum physics, reveals a deeply interwoven narrative about the nature of consciousness and its relationship to our divine identity.

The *Zohar* describes consciousness as a reflective process: *"A person is a mirror of the higher worlds."* This metaphor suggests that human awareness serves as both a receiver and transmitter of divine light. Consciousness becomes not just a passive experience but an active engagement with the divine structure of reality. Similarly, the *Sefer Yetzirah* elaborates on the divine architecture of existence, revealing consciousness as a creative and participatory force.

QUANTUM PHYSICS AND THE MYSTICAL PERSPECTIVE

Quantum physics provides a fascinating framework for understanding consciousness in terms of interconnectedness. The Copenhagen Interpretation suggests that particles exist in a state of probability until observed, implying that consciousness plays a role in shaping physical reality. This mirrors mystical traditions that emphasise the creative power of thought and intention. When consciousness is unlocked identity and substance can unfold.

For instance, the principle of *tikkun olam* (repairing the world) in Jewish mysticism resonates with the idea of participatory consciousness. According to Kabbalistic thought, humans have a role in restoring divine harmony by aligning their consciousness with divine will.

ENTANGLING OF PROTONS IN QUANTUM PHYSICS IS A PERFECT EXAMPLE OF CONSCIOUSNESS

Start with two protons (tiny particles that make up the nuclei of atoms) that are part but of the same hydrogen molecule. These two protons are placed in a special setup where their "spin" (a property that's like a tiny magnet pointing either up or down) becomes entangled. This means that the two protons are now linked in such a way that the spin of one is connected to the spin of the other, no matter how far apart they are.

Now, they carefully separate the two protons, moving them far away from each other, as in this example, they sent one proton into space. Despite the distance, their entanglement (consciousness) keeps them connected.

Here's where the magic of quantum physics comes in: Whatever they did to the proton on earth, the exact same happened to the one in space, as if they were not apart. This happens instantly, even though the protons are far apart. It's as if they "know" what's happening to each other, consciousness unlocked.

This experiment shows something incredible about how consciousness works. At the quantum level, particles can stay connected in ways that defy our usual understanding of distance and time. It closely ties in with the scripture 'As He is, so are we in this world'...as He is in the spirit so we are in the physical. Consciousness revealed is the force that unlocks in the spirit to manifest in the physical.

CONSCIOUSNESS, QUANTUM ENTANGLEMENT, AND CHRISTIAN MYSTICISM: THE DIVINE CONNECTION

The mystery of consciousness has intrigued humans for ages, as it is a fundamental part of our existence. Despite experiencing it constantly, we still struggle to fully understand its origins and essence. Is it simply a result of brain activity, or does it hold a deeper significance, possibly even divine, in nature? While modern science, particularly quantum physics, has delved into the interconnectedness of reality, Christian mysticism has long spoken of this unity. By exploring the concept of quantum entanglement, we may discover intriguing parallels with the teachings of Christian mystics who have long described a profound, non-local connection with God and all of creation.

QUANTUM ENTANGLEMENT AND THE UNITY OF ALL THINGS

In the realm of quantum physics, there is a phenomenon known as entanglement. It is a peculiar occurrence where two particles become inexorably intertwined, regardless of the distance that separates them as earlier discussed. Remarkably, any alteration in one particle instantaneously affects the other, even if vast cosmic expanses separate them. Scientists grapple with comprehending how this inexplicable connection transcends the boundaries of time and space. Its implications are profound, revealing a profound interconnectivity that permeates the very fabric of reality.

Let us now explore the implications of this concept for Christian mysticism. Throughout history, Christian mystics have shared their profound encounters with God, describing them as a dissolution of the self into something much greater. They often refer to this as a "Divine Indwelling", where God is not seen as an external entity but as a presence that is intimately intertwined with and transcends all things. In the book of Acts 17:28, St. Paul affirms this notion by stating, "For in Him we live and move and have our being." This idea resonates with the understanding that consciousness, similar to entangled particles, may not be limited to the physical body but part of a vast and interconnected spiritual reality. Thus, we can see the parallels between Mystical Union and the concept of the Quantum Soul.

Throughout history, Christian mysticism has placed great emphasis on the unio mystica, also known as the mystical union with God. Esteemed figures such as St. Teresa of Avila, St. John of the Cross, and Meister Eckhart have eloquently described profound encounters where the divisions between self and God appeared to vanish, revealing nothing but a state of pure awareness, love, and unity. Remarkably, this experience bears a resemblance to the notion of quantum non-locality, which suggests that reality is not confined by the constraints of space and time but intricately interconnected in ways that surpass our comprehension.

If we consider the concept of quantum entanglement, which suggests a mysterious interconnectedness among all things, it might explain why Christian mystics have always described an indescribable unity with God. It is possible that consciousness, at its most profound level, is not an isolated occurrence but a divine energy and frequency that is intricately intertwined with the Creator.

THE RESURRECTION AND THE CONTINUITY OF CONSCIOUSNESS

That a quantum approach to consciousness has profound implications is that it suggests consciousness may not be limited by physical death. In Christian faith, Jesus' resurrection is a pivotal event, showcasing that life goes beyond the confines of the physical body. Quantum theories propose that consciousness is non-local, so death is not the ultimate end of awareness. Instead, it is a transition into a greater and interconnected reality. This aligns with the concept of the Beatific Vision, a term used by Christian mystics to describe the direct encounter with God.

This aligns with John 11:25, Jesus's declaration: "I am the resurrection and the life." "The one who believes in me will live, even though they die." Mystics such as St. Catherine of Siena and St. Augustine described eternity not as a future event far away but as a current reality in which the soul can already experience a divine union. This serves as evidence that our consciousness, like entangled particles, is already connected to creation and its Creator, beyond the constraints of space and time.

PRAYER, MEDITATION, AND THE TUNING OF CONSCIOUSNESS

If consciousness is indeed a component of a greater divine interconnectedness, then prayer and contemplation can be viewed as methods of aligning oneself with this sacred existence. Throughout history, Christian mystics engaged in practices such as hesychasm, which entails cultivating inner stillness and contemplative meditation, a form of prayer that transcends verbal expression. These practices appear to facilitate an enhanced perception of Gods presence. Jesus Himself emphasised the significance of this in Matthew 6:6, urging individuals to engage in solitary, profound prayer by stating, "But when you pray, go into your room, close the door and pray to your Father, who is unseen."

The concept of observation and attention having the power to change reality itself is mirrored in quantum principles. When we consider prayer as divine observation, it becomes more than just a means to connect with God. It also serves to align our consciousness with the divine order, creating a tangible experience of what is referred to as the Kingdom of Heaven within (Luke 17:21).

THE CHRIST-CONSCIOUSNESS AND THE UNIFIED FIELD

The connection between quantum entanglement and Christian mysticism leads to a remarkable conclusion: consciousness has a fundamental nature that is divine, interconnected, and everlasting. In the Bible, Jesus likened Himself to a Vine and His followers to branches (John 15:5), highlighting a profound and living bond between all of creation and God. Christian mystics, much like quantum physicists, describe a universe where everything is intricately connected in an enigmatic and indivisible unity. It is possible that what science is currently uncovering—the profound entanglement of all things—is what Christian mystics have always understood: that we are not separate from creation and its Creator but exist within the boundless and loving consciousness of Christ. Through prayer, contemplation, and love, we awaken to this divine truth, realising that we are not isolated individuals but integral parts of an eternal communion with the Creator, akin to the quantum realm.

CONSCIOUSNESS IN THE BIBLICAL CONTEXT

The Bible offers a foundational perspective on consciousness as a reflection of humanity's unique relationship with God. In Genesis 2:7, we read: "Then the LORD God formed man of dust from the ground, and breathed into his nostrils the breath of life; and man became a living soul." (Man became aware).

This verse highlights two critical elements: the physical form (dust) and the divine breath (spirit). The "breath of life" (Hebrew: nishmat chayim) also serves as a metaphor for divine consciousness imparted to humanity. The term "living soul" (nephesh chayah) indicates a being capable of self-awareness, thought, and spiritual communion.

The Shema Yisrael in Deuteronomy 6:4 ("Hear, O Israel: The LORD our God, the LORD is one") further suggests a unified consciousness underlying creation. Mystical interpretations, such as those in the Kabbalah, view this unity as a profound oneness where individual consciousness mirrors the collective and Divine mind of God.

CONSCIOUSNESS IN MYSTICAL WRITINGS

Jewish mysticism, particularly the Kabbalistic tradition, delves deeply into the nature of consciousness. The **Tree of Life** is a central metaphor, depicting ten *sefirot* (emanations) through which divine energy flows into creation. These *sefirot* represent both cosmic principles and aspects of human consciousness, from the spiritual and intellectual realm (*Chokhmah*—wisdom and *Binah*—understanding) to the emotional and physical realms.

Similarly, Christian mysticism, as articulated by figures like Meister Eckhart, views consciousness as a point of divine encounter. Eckhart emphasised the "spark of the soul," a place where human awareness meets God. He wrote, "*The soul's highest function is not to think but to be open to God's light.*"

This echoes the idea that consciousness is not merely a mental activity but an openness to the transcendent, a divine entanglement that creates transference from the heavenly realms.

CONSCIOUSNESS AS DIVINE IMAGE

The concept of being made in the "image of God" found in Genesis 1:27 further illustrates consciousness as a reflection of the divine. To be created in God's image implies a capacity for divine self-awareness, creativity, and moral discernment, qualities that distinguish humanity from other forms of life.

Philo of Alexandria, a Jewish philosopher, saw the Imago Dei as the rational and spiritual aspect of human consciousness, which enables communion with Yahweh. Christian mystic Teilhard de Chardin took this a step further, suggesting that consciousness evolves toward a divine endpoint he called the Omega Point, where humanity unites with Christ in universal consciousness.

It is important to note that in other religions and new age practices, consciousness is the path to salvation. Have you heard of the phrase 'Christ Consciousness'? Well, it represents a mystical interpretation of Jesus's teachings that differs from Biblical Christianity in several key ways, and can be subtle:

CORE CONCEPT:

Christ Consciousness views the "Christ" as a state of divine consciousness or enlightenment that anyone can potentially achieve, rather than being only embodied in Jesus, the Son of God, the Word became flesh. It suggests that Jesus exemplified this state of consciousness but wasn't unique in having access to it.

KEY DIFFERENCES:

1. Nature of Jesus

Biblical: Jesus is uniquely divine, the singular Son of God, the Word became flesh that dwelt among men. He is the Son of God and therefore, God.

Christ Consciousness: Jesus was an enlightened master who showed the potential for human-divine unity that all can achieve.

2. Path to Salvation

Biblical: Through faith in Jesus Christ as personal saviour and the work of the cross. Christ is the way, the truth and the life.

Christ Consciousness: Through expanding one's consciousness to achieve higher states of spiritual awareness.

Now, as a mystic, that's exactly what we do, but our ascension pathway attaining higher states of consciousness is through embracing the finished work of the cross of Jesus Christ and its lifestyle, not just being aware of it.

3. Individual's Relationship to Divinity

Biblical: Humans as sons of God were separate from Him because of the fall, therefore requiring mediation through Christ's death and resurrection. Embracing Jesus reinstates us to our rightful place as sons of God, seated in heavenly realms.

Christ Consciousness: Through spiritual development and unlocking consciousness, humans can realise their inherent divinity.

The Bible depicts Christ as a person who is also God. Christ's consciousness, He is a force or a cosmic presence. Some Christian mystics speak of Christ's Consciousness. It is, however, from a place of recognition, Christ's presence and power within us and the realms He possesses in and through us.

MEDITATION AND CONSCIOUSNESS

Meditation serves as a bridge between human and divine consciousness. Both Jewish and Christian mysticism emphasise practices that quiet the mind and attune the soul to God's presence. In the Psalms, David writes: "Be still, and know that I am God" (Psalm 46:10).

This "stillness" reflects the meditative state where self dissolves, allowing one to experience the deeper reality of divine unity. Jewish meditation often involves contemplation on the *Divine Name* (*YHVH*) or focusing on the light emanating from God. Christian contemplative prayer, as taught by saints like Teresa of Avila, involves a similar journey inward to the "interior castle" where God resides.

ASCENSION AND THE EXPANSION OF CONSCIOUSNESS

The idea of ascension, found in both mystical and biblical narratives, symbolises the expansion of consciousness toward divine realms. The story of Jacob's ladder in Genesis 28:12 portrays a vision of angels ascending and descending between heaven and earth, a metaphor for the interplay between higher and lower states of awareness.

The New Testament also speaks to the transformative potential of consciousness. In Philippians 2:5, Paul writes, "Let this mind be in you, which was also in Christ Jesus." This "mind of Christ" signifies a state of consciousness aligned with divine love, wisdom, and humility.

CONSCIOUSNESS AND UNITY

Central to both mystical and quantum perspectives is the notion of interconnectedness. Jesus' prayer in **John 17:21**—"*that they may all be one, just as you, Father, are in me, and I in you*"—reflects a vision of unity where individual consciousness participates in the collective divine reality.

The Kabbalistic concept of *Ein Sof* (the Infinite) parallels this idea. *Ein Sof* represents the limitless and undifferentiated divine consciousness from which all things emanate. Mystics believe that by aligning their awareness with the *Ein Sof*, they transcend individual limitations and experience oneness with the Creator.

PRACTICAL IMPLICATIONS: CONSCIOUSNESS AND GROUNDING

Grounding consciousness involves cultivating a harmonious balance between spiritual awareness and earthly responsibilities. Mystical practices such as prayer, meditation, and acts of compassion help integrate divine consciousness into daily life.

In quantum terms, grounding can be likened to the "collapse of the wave function," where potential becomes reality. By aligning intention with divine will, individuals can manifest higher states of being, contributing to the healing of themselves and the world.

CONCLUSION: CONSCIOUSNESS AS DIVINE COMMUNION

Consciousness is both a gift and a responsibility, offering humanity the potential to participate in the divine mystery. Rooted in the biblical narrative and enriched by mystical traditions, it serves as a bridge between the finite and the infinite.

As the apostle Paul wrote in 1 Corinthians 2:16, "For who has known the mind of the Lord so as to instruct him? But we have the mind of Christ."

This "mind of Christ" invites believers to transcend egoic limitations, embrace divine wisdom, and co-create with God in the unfolding of creation.

Ultimately, consciousness is not merely an individual phenomenon but a cosmic reality, a reflection of the divine unity that permeates all existence. It is in stillness, prayer, and the practice of love that we truly come to know the depth of this mystery, realising that, as the mystics affirm, "God is closer to us than our own soul."

This exploration is only a glimpse into the rich interplay between theology, mysticism, and modern science. Each path offers unique insights, yet they converge on the profound truth that consciousness is a sacred gift—a call to awaken to our divine potential and to participate in the restoration and transformation of the world.

... a spiritual practice and a means of connecting with Yahweh

Mystic Meditation

MEDITATION IN MYSTICISM: ORIGINS, SIGNIFICANCE, AND SACRED TEXTS

Meditation plays a central role in Christian mysticism, serving as both a spiritual practice and a means of connecting with Yahweh. Mystics have long used meditative practices to seek direct and transformative experiences within the realms they occupy in Christ. Similarly, the origins of meditation in Jewish mysticism can be traced back to the seeds found in the Hebrew Bible. The term for meditation in Hebrew, hitbodedut (התבודדות), translates to "self-seclusion" or "isolation," indicating a practice of withdrawal. Examples of contemplative prayer and meditation can be seen in King David's psalms, providing some of the earliest instances of such practices.

In Psalm 1:2, the righteous are described as those who meditate on the word day and night: "But his delight is in the law of the Lord, and in His law he meditates day and night."

In Philippians 4:8, Paul instructs believers to focus their thoughts meditatively: "Finally, brethren, whatever things are true, whatever things are noble, whatever things are just, whatever things are pure... meditate on these things."

Here, meditation is associated with a deep, repetitive engagement with sacred words and teachings. This focus on scripture as a source of meditation finds continuity in later Jewish mystical traditions. In the prophetic tradition, Elijah's encounter with the "still small voice" on Mount Horeb (1 Kings 19:12) illustrates the contemplative pursuit of subtle divine revelation. Instead of encountering God in the wind, earthquake, or fire, Elijah perceives God in a moment of profound stillness. This notion of quiet, inward listening anticipates the later contemplative methods found in mysticism.

MEDITATION IN EARLY JEWISH MYSTICAL TEXTS

The earliest texts of Jewish mysticism, such as the Sefer Yetzirah (The Book of Creation), offer frameworks for meditative and mystical contemplation. The Sefer Yetzirah presents a cosmology based on the interplay of the 22 Hebrew letters and the 10 Sefirot (emanations). Meditation on these letters and numbers, combined with focused visualisation and contemplation, leading to an understanding of the divine mysteries of creation.

Sefer Yetzirah reflects this practice: "Ten Sefirot of Nothingness... Their measure is ten, yet they have no end. Their limit is infinite. Their boundary is to the uttermost. And He is the Master of the Universe." (1:4)

The Hekhalot literature, texts dating from the Talmudic period (3rd-7th centuries CE), also features meditative techniques. These texts describe the mystical ascent to heavenly palaces or Hekhalot. The journey involves mental preparation, prayer, and engaging ecstatic states, enabling the mystic to engage the throne.

PSEUDEPIGRAPHA AND APOCRYPHAL INSIGHTS

The Book of Enoch, a key piece of Jewish apocalyptic literature, describes Enoch's heavenly journeys, during which he contemplates divine mysteries. Enoch's meditative ascent reveals a yearning for intimate knowledge of the celestial realms.

In the Apocalypse of Abraham (1st-2nd century CE), Abraham experiences a visionary ascent following a period of meditative reflection and sacrifice:

"I stood still, and I saw a fiery chariot with fiery wheels... And the angel said, 'Abraham, contemplate the expanse of heaven.'"

This contemplative vision underscores meditation as a gateway to divine knowledge and theophany.

SIGNIFICANCE OF MEDITATION IN MYSTICAL TRADITIONS

In Jewish meditation, there is a strong emphasis on devekut (דבקות), which refers to "clinging" to God and experiencing a profound connection with His presence. Similarly, Christian mysticism, particularly during the medieval period, pursued a mystical union with God, through meditative prayer.

Ultimately, meditation is not just a practice but a lifestyle, a luminous ascent into the corridors of divine consciousness. It is the sacred threshold where soul and body entwine, igniting the celestial inheritance within. To meditate is to pierce the veil, to be drawn into the secret caverns of Yahweh, where primordial light seeks to make itself known in the sanctum of the heart.

Recollection is far more than passive stillness; it is a hallowed alchemy of gathering the scattered sparks of the soul, drawing them into a singular radiance. Like the sacred art of Kabbalistic Tikkun, where the fractured vessels of being are reconstituted in divine harmony, so too does Recollection summon the fragmented self into the wholeness of divine presence. It is the work of gathering, of drawing breath into the eternal now, of resting the mind upon the ineffable name of Yahweh that vibrates within all things. Whether through the steady rhythm of sacred breath, or the incantatory repetition of a divine utterance, the purpose remains steadfast—to return to the Centre, the still point where the spirit is enveloped in the divine embrace. Therein lies the mystery: to persist in stillness is to transmute into the stepping stones of ascent. The ancient sage Evagrius of Pontus speaks with piercing clarity: "Someone who is tied up cannot run." So too, the intellect that remains shackled by restless desires and insatiable cravings is bound, unable to take flight into the spiritual domain of mystical prayer.

As the soul deepens into this practice, a great unveiling occurs. The illusions of excess, the mirage of endless striving, the clamour of worldly ambition—they all dissolve in the purifying fire of contemplation. We awaken to the great and simple truth: God alone sustains us. The frantic hunger of the modern age, with its ceaseless grasping and perpetual distraction, fades before the revelation that all things are held in the hands of God. In this sacred stillness, we learn the forgotten art of relinquishment, the holy science of release.

Recollection does not simplify; it illuminates. In this luminous emptiness, all that is unnecessary falls away, and what remains is the essential: the soul standing unveiled before the Beloved. This is the threshold of transformation, the portal to the mystical ascent, where self and Source become indistinguishable in the luminous depth of divine Love. Recollection is not an end but a beginning, the door through which one must pass to enter the sacred spiral of ever-deepening union with Yahweh. It reveals not just what we can let go of, but what we need to entangle with. In the stillness of Recollection, we discern the presence of God, and through this discernment, we prepare ourselves for the deeper transformative work ahead.

CONTEMPLATION AS THE GATEWAY TO DIVINE UNION

In her seminal work, The Interior Castle, Teresa of Ávila unveils a vision of the soul as a resplendent, crystalline castle fashioned from the purest diamond. This celestial dwelling shimmers with divine light, its many mansions forming the sacred architecture of the mystical journey. At the heart of this castle lies the innermost sanctuary, the Holy of Holies, where the Divine Presence dwells in eternal radiance. This is the sacred space of consummate union, the point of deepest intimacy where the soul, having shed all illusion, awakens to the eternal embrace of the Beloved.

Embarking on this journey is an inward pilgrimage of ascension, a spiralling movement that entangles into the depths of divine intimacy. As the outer mansions are encountered, they serve as thresholds of awakening, where the soul is stirred by the whisper of intimacy. Here, humility acts as the initial lantern, shedding light on the path through prayer and self-examination. Within the contemplation chambers, you gradually discerns the divine spark, not merely as an abstract notion but as a tangible, living presence.

ENTERING THE FOURTH MANSION

As the soul ventures deeper, the nature of the journey transforms. Upon crossing the threshold of the fourth mansion, a luminous shift occurs: the journey is no longer propelled by mere human effort but by the unseen currents of the Holy Spirit. Striving yields to surrender, effort dissolves into trust, and the ego relinquishes its grip. It is no longer the seeker who moves but the Spirit who moves the seeker. This is the threshold of contemplation, where prayer transcends words and gives way to silence, a silence that is not emptiness but fullness beyond speech.

Teresa likens this unfolding to a divine dance, a celestial choreography where the soul learns to yield to the Spirit's lead. The rhythm is one of surrender and consent, an intimate attunement to the subtle movements of grace. Here, God ceases to be the distant Other and is known as the One in whom we live, move, and have our being.

THE PRAYER OF SILENT PRESENCE

Contemplative prayer is the soul's gentle surrender into divine stillness. It is not grasping for God but the resting in God. It is the prayer of quiet, the awareness beyond thought, beyond image, where the spirit is drawn into the depths of divine presence. In this silent communion, the veil of separation disappears, and the soul perceives itself as already held, already known, already one with Yahweh.

In this sacred stillness, the contemplative discovers that silence is not absence but presence, a presence that envelopes, transforms, and beckons ever deeper. As the Psalmist declares, "Be still and know that I am God." This knowing is not intellectual but experiential, a deep recognition that unfolds in the silent chambers of the heart.

THE SACRED GROUND OF CONTEMPLATION

The very word contemplation carries within it the whisper of the sacred. Stemming from the Latin 'contemplare', meaning "to observe with reverence," and 'templum', denoting a consecrated space, contemplation is the act of stepping into the inner sanctuary where God abides. The human heart becomes the temple, the meeting place between the finite and the Infinite, the visible and the ineffable.

Christian mysticism has long understood that this inward temple mirrors the Holy of Holies, the place where divine glory dwells. The practice of contemplation, then, is nothing less than the soul's return to its true dwelling place, a homecoming into the vast stillness where the Eternal waits in loving silence, dancing to the frequencies of remembrance. God is no longer sought in visions or consolations but is found in the naked reality of the present moment. In the seeming emptiness, the fullness of divine presence is revealed.

SURRENDER, THE ESSENCE OF CONTEMPLATIVE PRAYER

The core of contemplative prayer lies in complete surrender. In moments of ecstasy or when seeking mystical experiences, there is a beauty in quietly surrendering oneself to God. Thomas Merton emphasises that "the gate of heaven is everywhere," suggesting that contemplation is accessible to all who are willing to enter into the silence.

In a world saturated with noise, this call to stillness is revolutionary. The endless hum of technology, the ceaseless demands of modern life, and the restless currents of the mind create formidable barriers to silence. Yet the contemplative is one who chooses, again and again, to return to the quiet centre. Even when distractions arise, the act of gently turning back to silence is itself an act of prayer. In this simple return, grace meets us.

THE THREEFOLD PATH OF CONTEMPLATION: DISCERNMENT, RECOGNITION, AND ACKNOWLEDGMENT

Evelyn Underhill articulates a threefold deepening of contemplation:

Discernment – The first awakening, where the soul learns to perceive the divine in all things. This is the moment of seeing—not with physical eyes, but with the eyes of the heart.

Recognition – A deeper awareness that God is both immanent and transcendent. Here, the soul begins to embrace the paradox of divine mystery.

Acknowledgement – The final surrender, where the soul relinquishes the need to grasp or understand and simply consents to being held in divine love.

This journey is not one of mastery but of surrender. Contemplation is not an achievement but a yielding, an allowing, a resting in the One who has always already been present.

THE INVITATION INTO SILENCE

Ultimately, contemplation is the invitation to step beyond the veil of illusion into the luminous stillness of divine presence. It is the call to rest in the eternal embrace, to listen to the unspoken Word, to dwell in the heart of the mystery. And as we surrender to this silence, we come to see that what we once called emptiness is, in truth, the fullness of God. The contemplative path unfolds, ever deeper, ever inward, until silence itself becomes the very language of love.

... direct access to spiritual elevation.

The Mystery of the Hebrew Language and Its Letters: Origins, Mysticism, and Foundational Role

The Hebrew language, known as the oldest tongue still in use today, possesses an inherent mystical essence that has captivated scholars, sages, and those in pursuit of divine wisdom for countless ages. Beyond mere means of communication, Hebrew is regarded as the very foundation of existence, a channel through which the essence of Yahweh materialises in our reality. Its roots, intricately intertwined with biblical creation, and its significance in mystical traditions, establish it as a fundamental pillar of spiritual exploration.

Hebrew, being a Semitic language, has its origins in the ancient Near East. The Torah regards Hebrew as the Lashon HaKodesh ("Holy Tongue"), implying that it was the original language spoken by Adam, the first human, and used by God to bring the universe into existence. According to Jewish tradition, the world itself was spoken into being through the divine words uttered in Hebrew. The Hebrew phrase "And God said..." precedes each Genesis creation act (e.g., "Let there be light"), demonstrating its generative capacity beyond mere description. Hebrew creates before it communicates.

The idea is further supported by the Sefer Yetzirah (Book of Creation), one of the oldest Kabbalistic texts known, which attributes the creation of the universe to the manipulation of Hebrew letters. The Aleph-Bet's twenty-two letters are not mere symbols but dynamic forces and entities, each carrying spiritual meaning, vibrational energy, and creative power.

THE MYSTICAL POWER OF THE HEBREW LETTERS

The Hebrew letters are regarded as sacred, holding both numerical (gematria) and symbolic significance. In contrast to contemporary alphabets, where letters primarily serve as phonetic indicators, Hebrew letters possess multiple dimensions and act as conduits for divine wisdom. The form, numerical value, and phonetic sound of each letter conceal profound meanings that mystics and scholars have diligently explored for centuries.

For instance:

Aleph (א) represents unity and divine transcendence. Its silent nature suggests the ineffable aspect of God's wonders.

Bet (ב), the first letter of the Torah (Bereshit), signifies creation and duality—Heaven and Earth, male and female, the temple of manifestation

Shin (ש), with its three branches, embodies divine fire, the balance of forces, and the hidden mysteries of Yeshua.

The esoteric meaning of the letters is further enhanced by their combinations. The name of God, known as the Tetragrammaton (YHVH), consists of four letters (יהוה) and is regarded as extremely sacred. The Name symbolises the timeless essence of God, encompassing the entire past, present, and future. It represents what was, what is, and what will be.

THE ROLE OF HEBREW IN MYSTICISM

Hebrew holds a foundational role in Kabbalah, the mystical tradition of Judaism that delves into the depths of existence. Under mystic teachings, every Hebrew letter serves as a gate for divine energy, shaping the very essence of creation. The Zohar, a key Kabbalistic text, recounts the story of each letter appealing to God for the honour of being the primary force behind the act of creation.

The practice of meditation frequently incorporates the visualisation and arrangement of Hebrew letters to harmonise one's consciousness with divine truths and gateways. The technique called 'Tzeruf' is an ancient meditation practice mentioned in the Bible as "calling on the name of the Lord." It involves connecting with the individual Hebrew letters of the name and using letter permutation to achieve heightened levels of awareness. An illustrative example of this is found in meditating upon the names of God, including the 72-letter name derived from three consecutive verses in Exodus, which are believed to facilitate spiritual elevation.

Moreover, the concept of gematria, which involves the numerical analysis of Hebrew words, uncovers profound connections among ideas that may appear unrelated. A prime illustration of this is found in the Hebrew word for "life" (Chai, חי), which possesses a numerical value of 18, holding great significance in Jewish tradition. Through the intricate correlation between numbers and letters, a complex tapestry of symbolism is woven, enabling mystics to unravel enigmatic revelations from the divine.

WHY HEBREW IS FOUNDATIONAL TO MYSTICISM

The Hebrew language and its letters go beyond being just tools for communication; they serve as instruments of divine interaction. Hebrew is viewed as a bridge connecting the finite and the infinite, allowing humanity to grasp spiritual truths that go beyond ordinary perception. In terms of linguistic purity, Biblical Hebrew has maintained a distinct sanctity, unlike many languages that have undergone significant evolution. It is the language of the kingdom of heaven, making it indispensable in mystical practice.

Creation and Reality: The Hebrew letters are the building blocks of creation. By understanding their deeper meanings, one gains insight into existence itself.

Divine Names and Power: Hebrew serves as the key to unlocking divine energy. Whether through the recitation of Psalms, mystical prayers, or contemplation of divine names, Hebrew provides direct access to spiritual elevation.

The Hebrew language transcends being merely a historical relic; it is a vibrant frequency of divine wisdom, pulsating with life. Within its letters lie hidden the mysteries of creation, and its words possess the power to mould reality itself. To study Hebrew is to embark on a profound exploration of the sacred blueprint of the universe, establishing it as the fundamental cornerstone of mysticism and an everlasting gateway to comprehending the limitless realms of an ineffable God.

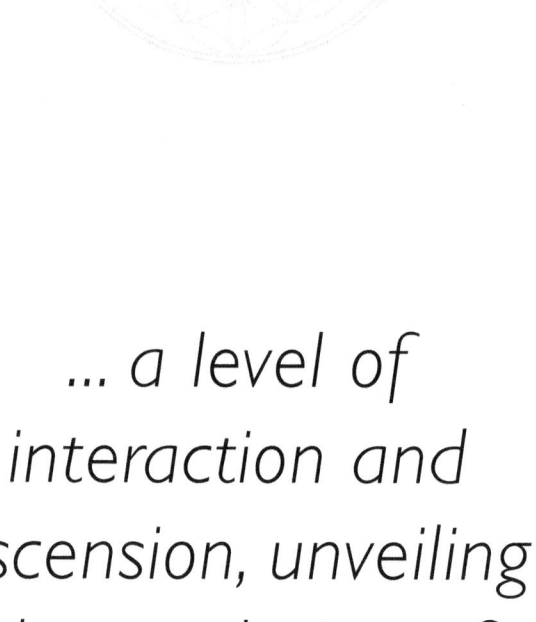

*... a level of
interaction and
ascension, unveiling
the revelation of
the Throne of God*

Merkavah Mysticism
- Light of Christ -
The Path of Ascent

Embarking on the Merkavah experience means stepping onto a path of fire and mystery, walked by ancient visionaries and mystics. The Prophet Ezekiel witnessed the chariot throne of God, a vision of thundering wheels, celestial fire creatures, and a radiant expanse where the Eternal Presence of Yahweh dwells. This vision was not just a sight but a mystical pathway - a portal to the mystical realms, structured and protected by angelic guardians. The Merkavah experience serves as an ascension journey, travelling through layers of spirituality, breaking through the veils of cosmic realms to reach the Throne of Glory. It symbolises the spirit's rise through contemplation, prayer, and sacred incantations.

For those who follow the light of Christ, Merkavah mysticism represents a fulfilled longing in the One who embodies both the heavenly chariot and the divine Rider. This mystical tradition reveals the ultimate mystery of God. Christ serves as the authentic path to ascent, a living gateway leading to the Holy of Holies. Here, the soul is not striving to reach God but is instead drawn into Him, undergoing transformation through the radiance of His presence.

ORIGINS AND FOUNDATIONS OF MERKAVAH MYSTICISM

The name Merkavah (מֶרְכָּבָה), meaning "chariot" in Hebrew, originates from the vision of the prophet Ezekiel (Ezekiel 1). In his revelation, the heavens parted to reveal a throne of sapphire, wheels within wheels, the four living creatures, and a multitude of fiery, angelic beings moving with divine intent. This is not just a vision but an invitation, a call to rise into the enigmatic radiance of God's presence.

Over time, a mystical tradition developed from a vision that gained prominence during the Second Temple period. Those on this path sought more than just pondering Ezekiel's vision; they aimed to actually experience its revelations. Their aspiration was to be transported into heavenly realms and journey through the seven celestial palaces described in the esoteric Hekhalot literature, also known as 3 Enoch. These ancient texts portray a mystical ascent through divine chambers, encountering angelic guardians, sacred fires, and uncovering the mysteries of the Kavod. These texts serve as guides, documenting the experiences of those who delve into divine revelation. Each angelic structure and obstacle symbolises a level of interaction and ascension, unveiling the revelation of the Throne of God.

For the Christian mystic, the journey no longer requires the soul to navigate the realms of the unseen alone. In Christ, the heavens are opened, and the throne is not distant; it is inside, dwelling within the believer. The vision of the chariot shifts from being a display of performance and striving to becoming an ascension towards unity and unlocking position and inheritance. Here, the mystic is not only a seer but is also seen, recognised, and embraced in the eternal inheritance as sons of God.

MERKAVAH TEXTS AND EARLY WRITINGS

The body of literature associated with Merkavah mysticism consists primarily of the Hekhalot (Palaces) texts. These writings, composed between the 3rd and 7th centuries CE, describe the journey of the mystic through seven heavenly palaces to reach the throne of God. Notable texts include:

1. Hekhalot Rabbati (Greater Palaces) – Provides detailed instructions for the ascension and encounters with angelic gatekeepers.

2. Hekhalot Zutarti (Lesser Palaces) – Offers descriptions of the heavenly realms and practical guidance for achieving visionary experiences.

3. Ma'aseh Merkavah (The Work of the Chariot) – Discusses the mystical interpretation of Ezekiel's vision and the ecstatic practices associated with it.

OTHER SCRIPTURAL INFLUENCES INCLUDE:

1. Isaiah 6 – The prophet's vision of the heavenly throne surrounded by seraphim, who cry out, "Holy, holy, holy is the Lord Almighty; the whole earth is full of his glory."

2. Exodus 24 – Moses' ascent on Mount Sinai and his encounter with God amidst a consuming cloud and fire.

3. Daniel 7 – The vision of the Ancient of Days seated on a fiery throne.

These passages suggested to ancient mystics that direct

encounters with Yahweh were possible through ecstatic ascent and visionary experiences.

It is crucial to recognise that while some texts offer profound insights into mystery and revelation, as a Christ-centred mystic, all our works are accomplished through Jesus and his finished work on the cross. Therefore, we should not focus on rituals and purification, as our true accomplishment lies in the body and blood of Jesus.

THE PROCESS AND FRAMEWORK OF MERKAVAH ASCENT

THE INFLUENCE OF THE ZOHAR

The Zohar, composed in the 13th century by the Spanish-Jewish mystic Moses de León, builds upon the foundations of Merkavah mysticism. The Zohar is a primary text of Kabbalah and blends Merkavah themes with a more developed mystical cosmology. It explores the divine emanations (sefirot) and the concept of the mystic's union with the Infinite (Ein Sof). The Zohar interprets the chariot as a dynamic symbol of the inner workings of divinity and the path toward divine intimacy. In the Zohar, the concept of the Shekinah (the indwelling feminine presence of God) adds a relational dimension to the otherwise ecstatic and transcendental aspects of Merkavah mysticism.

I've set out below a basic structure of Merkavah mysticism. It can vary to a great degree and is personalised based on a relationship with Jesus.

CHRISTIAN MYSTICISM AND MERKAVAH INFLUENCE

Merkavah mysticism significantly influenced Christian mysticism, particularly in the early and medieval periods. Several factors contributed to this cross-pollination of ideas:

1. Ezekiel's vision in Christian Thought – Christian mystics and theologians, such as Origen and Gregory the Great, interpreted Ezekiel's vision as a metaphor for the soul's ascent to God. The chariot symbolised a journey toward divine contemplation.

2. The Heavenly Ascent Motif – Christian mystics like Pseudo-Dionysius the Areopagite expanded on the concept of ascending through hierarchical orders of angels, mirroring the Merkavah's ascent through heavenly palaces. The notion of purification, illumination, and union reflects the stages of Merkavah mysticism.

3. Mystical Ecstasy and Vision – Meister Eckhart, Hildegard of Bingen, and St. Teresa of Ávila engaged in ecstatic experiences similar to Merkavah practices. Teresa's description of her mystical ascent in the Interior Castle parallels the heavenly ascent through progressive stages of spiritual purification.

4. The Chariot as Christological Symbol – In Christian mysticism, the chariot is allegorised as a symbol of Christ's Incarnation, carrying humanity toward divine glory. This Christological interpretation imbued Merkavah themes with distinctly Christian significance represented by the man (Christ) in the midst of the Throne.

5. The Visionary Tradition – The emphasis on direct, unmediated visions of God aligns with Christian mystical traditions of contemplative prayer, where the mystic seeks divine intimacy beyond rational comprehension.

STEP ONE: POSITIONING

1. Purification of Intent

Set your intention clearly: Why do you seek to ascend? Are you driven by reverence, a yearning for wisdom, or the desire to draw deeper into Yahweh?

2. Sacred Fast and Cleansing

The ancient mystics used to perform purification rituals, such as fasting, immersing in natural waters (mikvah), and avoiding worldly distractions. They believed that a calm body would allow the soul to awaken. Jesus underwent that on the cross for our sake. Our connection to Jesus is our pathway to spiritual closeness and purification.

3. Establishing Sacred Space

Find a place that brings you peace. Personally, I enjoy using essential oils to create an atmosphere that reflects my intimate space with Jesus.

4. Invocation and Chanting

Sacred names hold power. Begin with blessings, praises, and sacred chants to attune yourself to the divine frequencies. The chanting of the names of God or the Hebrew letters. It creates a resonance that positions you for ascension.

STEP TWO: ENTERING THE CHARIOT

To ascend, the mystic employs focused meditation, visualisation, and deep rhythmic breathing to unlock the gateways of perception.

1. The Throne of the Heart

Close your eyes and breathe deeply and evenly. Envision a throne of sapphire light, glowing with an inner fire and pulsating with life. This is the throne from which your spirit will ascend. Sense its energy grow as you continue to breathe.

2. The Ascent Begins

Inhale the light, exhale the distractions. With each breath, feel yourself ascending. The world fades around you as you transcend the physical realm, lifted by your inner longing. A majestic storm cloud materialises in front of you, illuminating with celestial flames.

Embrace this experience. It is the whirlwind around the chariot Throne, the gateway to elevated dimensions. Take a step forward. Engage with what you experience and allow the Holy Spirit to guide you through the experience.

Merkavah in the Light of Christ

Merkavah mysticism is a profound exploration of the human desire for divine encounter and transformation. It developed into a structured mystical framework emphasising spiritual ascent, ecstatic union, and the transformative power of beholding the divine glory. Its echoes in Christian mysticism reflect a shared longing across religious traditions to experience the ineffable and transcendent mystery of God. Through its rich imagery, esoteric practices, and heavenly aspirations, Merkavah mysticism continues to inspire mystics on the path toward divine intimacy and spiritual enlightenment.

For Christians, Merkavah mysticism is not a separate or alien path but a foreshadowing of the true ascent made possible in Jesus Christ. Early Christian mystics perceived Christ as the realisation of Ezekiel's vision – the enthroned King, the chariot of Glory, the genuine ladder through which we ascend into the realms of His presence (John 1:51). In Christ, the path of Merkavah mysticism finds its culmination not through hidden knowledge or angelic codes, but through the living way He has unveiled through His sacrifice (Hebrews 10:20). Although we can ascend and explore the seven palaces in the kingdom, a truly remarkable experience, it is through the completed work of the cross that we discover our access and entrance in Christ, in whom the entire fullness of God dwells in bodily form (Colossians 2:9), the High Priest who has passed through the heavens (Hebrews 4:14).

In Christ, the Merkavah experience is truly extraordinary, available for all who embrace the finished work of the cross, a privilege to engage in heavenly structure. A true adventure.

*... exists within the
human soul and
body, making them
a bridge between
God and humanity.*

Kabbalah: Origins, Purpose, and Structure

If there's one word that makes Christians uneasy, it is 'Kabbalah'. This Hebrew term, קַבָּלָה (pronounced as written), originates from the root 'ק-ב-ל' (Q-B-L), which means "to receive" or "accept." It denotes a "received tradition" or "that which is handed down," representing the esoteric, mystical aspect of Judaism. While it formally appeared in medieval times, its origins can be traced back to early Jewish mystical ideas such as Merkavah (Chariot) mysticism from the Talmudic era (1st–6th centuries CE) and Hekhalot literature (Palace Mysticism). The structured form of Kabbalah emerged in the 12th–13th centuries, leading to works like Sefer ha-Bahir and Sefer ha-Zohar (the Book of Splendour), often linked to Rabbi Shimon bar Yochai. For Christians, the questions often asked are: Is the term 'Kabbalah' mentioned in the Bible and is it a new age practice?

In its specific sense as a mystical tradition, the word 'Kabbalah' does not appear in the Hebrew Bible (Tanakh). Biblical texts show ק-ב-ל root variations used differently, generally meaning "receive" or "accept".

1. Exodus 26:5

Hebrew: וַחֲמִשִּׁים קַרְסֵי זָהָב וְחִבַּרְתָּ אֶת־הַיְרִיעֹת אִשָּׁה אֶל־אֲחֹתָהּ בַּקְּרָסִים וְהָיָה הַמִּשְׁכָּן אֶחָד:

Translation: "And you shall make fifty clasps of gold, and **couple** the curtains to one another with the clasps so that the tabernacle may be one."

The term לְקַבֵּל (le-kabel) appears in this context, meaning "to couple" or "to join."

2. Proverbs 19:20

Hebrew: שְׁמַע עֵצָה וְקַבֵּל מוּסָר לְמַעַן תֶּחְכַּם בְּאַחֲרִיתֶךָ:

Translation: "Listen to advice **and accept** instruction, so that you may gain wisdom in the future."

Here, וְקַבֵּל (ve-kabel) means "and accept."

The purpose of Kabbalah is to reveal the hidden dimensions of God's relationship with creation, explore the structure of divine reality, and guide human beings toward spiritual enlightenment and closeness to the Ein Sof (the Infinite). It provides mystical interpretations of the Torah and aims to help practitioners achieve devekut (דבקות), or cleaving to God.

THE TREE OF LIFE'S SEFIROT (NAMED CIRCLES)

The Tree of Life is the central mystical diagram in Kabbalah, representing the structure of the divine emanations (sefirot). No, it doesn't replace Jesus, who is THE TREE OF LIFE. It functions as a map of divine energy flowing from God (the top), into the world (the bottom), and serves as both a cosmic structure and a spiritual path for personal transformation.

THE TEN SEFIROT: THE DIVINE EMANATIONS

The sefirot (סְפִירוֹת) are ten aspects or attributes through which God interacts with creation. They are both aspects of divine manifestation and levels of consciousness that a mystic aligns with to reach higher states of unity with God.

The ten sefirot are divided into three columns (right, left, and centre), representing different modes of divine flow:

Keter (Crown) – The infinite divine will; beyond human comprehension.

Chokhmah (Wisdom) – The initial spark of creative inspiration.

Binah (Understanding) – The development and structuring of wisdom.

Chesed (Loving-Kindness) – Boundless love and expansion.

Gevurah (Strength, Judgment) – Divine discipline and restraint.

Tiferet (Beauty, Harmony) – Balance between love and judgment; divine compassion.

Netzach (Eternity, Victory) – Endurance, perseverance, and divine flow.

Hod (Splendour, Glory) – Humility and divine receptivity.

Yesod (Foundation) – The bridge between divine energy and the physical world.

Malkhut (Kingdom) – The divine presence (Shekinah) in the material world.

HOW THE SEFIROT WORK: A DEEPER UNDERSTANDING

The sefirot function as a dynamic and interactive system of divine energy that governs both the cosmos and the human soul. They serve as channels through which God's presence is manifested in creation, and they reflect the process of divine emanation from the highest, most transcendent level to the most immanent and earthly reality.

THE FLOW OF DIVINE ENERGY: HISHTALSHELUT (THE CHAIN OF EMANATION)

The flow of divine energy through the sefirot is guided by a structured descent called Hishtalshelut (השתלשלות, "the chain of emanation"). This process is designed to gradually filter and adapt the infinite light of Ein Sof (the Infinite God) so that it can be perceived and sustained by the finite world. Without this filtration, the power and energy would be too overwhelming and would dissolve creation.

THIS DESCENT UNFOLDS IN THE FOLLOWING STAGES:

Keter (Crown) – The first and most subtle stage, representing Gods divine will before it takes form. Keter is like a seed of infinite potential, containing all possible realities in an undifferentiated form.

Chokhmah (Wisdom) – The initial flash of inspiration, akin to a lightning bolt, where divine wisdom bursts into existence. It is raw, undefined insight.

Binah (Understanding) – The structuring and development of Chokhmah's insight. Here, wisdom is analysed, categorised, and made comprehensible.

Chesed (Loving-Kindness) – The first manifestation of divine flow into the world, expressing limitless giving, love, and expansion.

Gevurah (Strength, Judgment) – The counterbalance to Chesed, imposing restriction, discipline, and judgment to ensure divine energy is not overwhelming.

Tiferet (Beauty, Harmony) – The integration of Chesed and Gevurah, bringing a balance between expansion and limitation, justice and mercy.

Netzach (Eternity, Victory) – The driving force of endurance and persistence, representing divine initiative and action in sustaining creation.

Hod (Splendour, Glory) – The receptive counterpart to Netzach, associated with humility, surrender, and the passive aspects of divine interaction.

Yesod (Foundation) – The bridge between the upper sefirot and the material world, channeling divine energy in a way that is accessible and manifest.

Malkhut (Kingdom) – The final stage where divine energy fully enters and sustains the physical world. It represents Shekinah, the immanent divine presence in creation.

This process of descent mirrors the story of creation in Genesis, where God speaks the world into existence through a gradual unfolding of order from chaos.

CORRESPONDENCE TO THE HUMAN SOUL AND BODY

Kabbalah teaches that the sefirot not only describes divine processes but also exists within the human soul and body, making them a bridge between God and humanity.

The Human Soul (Nefesh, Ruach, Neshamah) Each person possesses a tripartite soul that corresponds to different levels of the sefirotic structure:

Nefesh (Vital Soul) – The lowest level, tied to physical life and instinct (corresponding to Malkhut and Yesod).

Ruach (Spirit) – The emotional and moral dimension of the soul associated with the middle sefirot (Chesed through Yesod).

Neshamah (Divine Soul) – The highest, most intellectual and spiritual aspect of the soul, linked to the upper sefirot (Keter, Chokhmah, Binah).

The Human Body, the sefirot is mapped onto the human form, reinforcing the idea that a person is a microcosm of the divine order:

Chesed (Right Arm) – Acts of kindness, giving.

Gevurah (Left Arm) – Restraint, discipline.

Tiferet (Torso/Heart) – Compassion, balance.

Netzach and Hod (Legs) – Movement, perseverance, humility.

Yesod (Genital Area) – Creativity, transmission of divine flow.

Malkhut (Feet/Presence in the World) – Action, grounding divine purpose in reality.

THE COSMIC DIMENSION OF THE SEFIROT

On the macrocosmic level, the sefirot also governs different aspects of creation. Each sefirah is associated with:

The heavens and celestial spheres governing the structure of the universe.

The elements of nature (fire, water, air, earth).

The flow of time and divine providence.

Harmonising the Sefirot Through Mystical Practice

A kabbalist studies the sefirot and actively engages in practices to harmonise them within themselves and within the world. These include:

Meditation – Contemplating the sefirotic structure, visualising divine light descending through the tree of life.

Prayer – Praying with Kavanah (deep intention), aligning one's consciousness with the divine flow.

Ethical Refinement – Developing inner virtues that correspond to the sefirot, such as balancing love and discipline in one's life.

Yichudim – Chanting divine names and performing sacred visualisations to merge different sefirotic energies and restore cosmic harmony.

Tikkun Olam (Repairing the World) – Engaging in acts of kindness and justice to elevate the divine presence in creation.

Through these practices, the Kabbalist serves as a conduit for divine light, participating in the ongoing process of creation and restoring unity between the spiritual and physical realms.

THE PURPOSE AND MEANING OF THE HEBREW LETTERS CONNECTING THE SEFIROT

The Hebrew letters that connect the sefirot in the 'Tree of Life' carry deep mystical significance. In Kabbalah, the Hebrew alphabet is considered primordial, meaning that the letters themselves are vessels of divine energy that shape creation.

THE HEBREW LETTERS AS CHANNELS OF DIVINE ENERGY

Each letter that connects two sefirot represents a path or channel through which divine energy flows. These paths illustrate the relationships between the sefirot and how the divine attributes interact dynamically rather than existing in isolation. The letters are seen as bridges that transfer divine energy, much like nerves connecting organs or veins channeling blood in the human body.

These connections form a spiritual circuitry, allowing the Ein Sof (Infinite Divine Light) to flow through creation in a structured way.

THE 22 PATHS AND THEIR CORRESPONDENCE TO THE HEBREW ALPHABET

The Tree of Life consists of 10 sefirot and 22 connecting paths, corresponding to the 22 letters of the Hebrew alphabet. Each path represents:

- A transition of divine energy from one attribute to another.
- A state of consciousness or that a mystic passes through in their ascent toward divine union.
- A connection between different modes of divine expression in creation.

THESE 22 LETTERS ARE ALSO ASSOCIATED WITH:

- The 22 creative utterances through which God formed the universe (as understood from Genesis and Sefer Yetzirah).
- The 22 pathways in the human soul, reflecting different ways we experience reality.

THE LETTERS AND THEIR NUMERICAL, MYSTICAL MEANINGS

Each Hebrew letter also carries:

- A numerical value (gematria) that links it to deeper meanings.
- A symbolic meaning that provides insight into its function in the divine process.
- A sound vibration that, when chanted, is believed to activate divine energy.

For example:

- Aleph (א) connects Keter (Crown) and Chokhmah (Wisdom), representing the pure, unformed potential of divine thought.
- Bet (ב) connects Chokhmah (Wisdom) to Binah (Understanding), symbolising the structuring of divine insight into an ordered form.

- Tav (ת) connects Yesod (Foundation) and Malkhut (Kingdom), representing the completion of the divine flow into manifestation.

HEBREW LETTERS AS A PATH OF ASCENT

For a mystic, meditating on and chanting these Hebrew letters is a way of:

- Aligning oneself with the divine energy of Yahweh.

- Limbing the Tree of Life through intellectual and spiritual refinement.

- Restoring balance in creation by harmonising the sefirotic energies within. Engaging with the Hebrew letters has been an adventurous journey for me, unfolding realms of divine governance and my position in Christ. I absolutely love the Hebrew letters and the realms they open up.

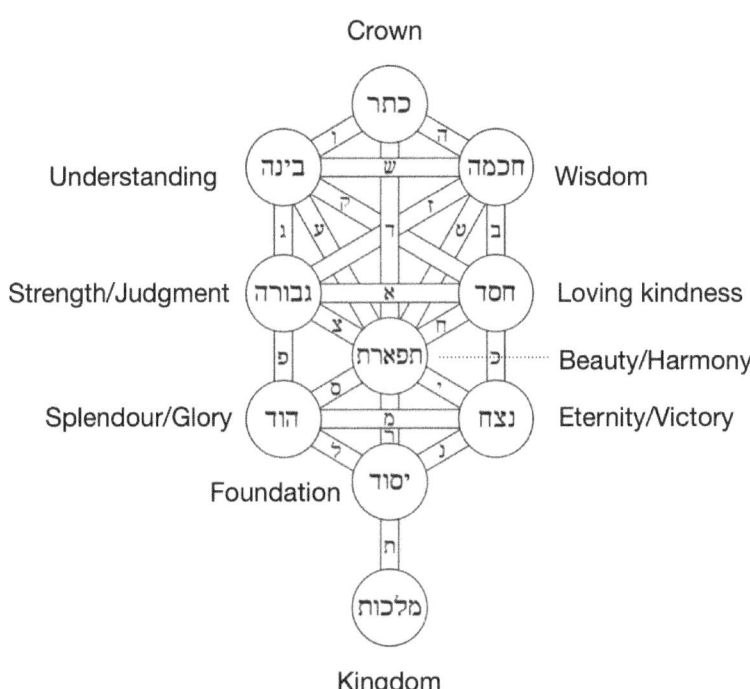

... breath becomes prayer and prayer becomes a vessel for divine indwelling

Breathing Techniques in Mysticism: Pathways to Altered States of Consciousness

Breath has been traditionally viewed as a sacred connection between the physical and the divine in Jewish and Christian mystical beliefs. It is seen not only as a biological process but as a spiritual instrument, allowing for deeper awareness and connection with God. It is the ability to bring about altered states of consciousness to attain spiritual enlightenment and states of ecstasy.

BREATH AND THE DIVINE

In both Jewish and Christian traditions, breath is closely associated with life and the presence of God. The Hebrew word ruach רוּחַ and the Greek pneuma πνεῦμα both signify "breath," "spirit," and "wind," reflecting the spiritual belief that breath is the vital force of existence. For example, in Genesis 2:7, God breathes life into Adam, symbolising the direct infusion of divinity into humanity through breath. Similarly, in John 20:22, Jesus breathes on his disciples and says, "Receive the Holy Spirit," highlighting the link between breath and divine inspiration. The Psalms and prophetic literature also underscore breath as a means of divine communication. Psalm 150:6 proclaims, "Let everything that has breath praise the Lord," implying that breath itself is an act of worship. The prophet Elijah encounters God not through fire or earthquake but in a "still small voice", which some mystical interpretations connect to the gentle rhythm of breath as a pathway to divine connection.

MYSTICISM CONTAINS RICH TEACHINGS ON BREATH CONTROL TO ACHIEVE MYSTICAL STATES

Breath is divine emanations that structure both the cosmos and the inner world of the soul. Meditation practices often involve visualisation and breath control to align oneself with these divine energies. A key technique, Hitbodedut (seclusion and meditative prayer), often includes controlled breathing to still the mind and attune to higher realities. This contemplative discipline harmonises the breath with the Word, aligning the inhalation and exhalation with the sacred rhythm of the Tetragrammaton (Yod-Heh-Vav-Heh, יהוה), the vibration of divine Being.

Each syllable of the Ineffable Name is not just a sound but a gateway into the emanations of the image of God, a mystical architecture through which the breath becomes a bridge between the finite and the Infinite. Yod ('), the primal spark and blueprint, is drawn inward with the inhale, a seed of divine wisdom planted in the depths of the soul. As the breath expands into Heh (ה), the sacred breath of creation, the mystic releases themselves into the vastness of divine presence. Vav (ו), the ascending and descending light, is felt in the breath's fullness, a vertical conduit connecting heaven and earth, spirit and form. Finally, Heh (ה) returns an exhalation of surrender, dissolving the self into the boundless expanse of God's ineffable love.

This practice is not merely a meditation, it is an alchemical process of transformation, where breath becomes prayer and prayer becomes a vessel for divine indwelling (Shekinah). The mystic, through rhythmic attunement, begins to dissolve the barriers of ego and separation, entering the silent expanse where God breathes through them. In this sacred alignment, the very act of breathing becomes a recitation of divine unfolding. Through sustained practice, the mystic becomes attuned to the subtle vibratory resonance hidden within the Name, uncovering the mystery that YHVH is not a word but a living breath, the very exhalation of God sustaining all existence. The breath itself is revealed as a secret prayer, an eternal whisper of divine intimacy, where one no longer simply recites the Name but becomes the Name.

HASIDIC BREATH PRACTICES: ECSTATIC DEVOTION

Rabbi Israel Baal Shem Tov taught that breath is a crucial element in prayer and connecting with Yahweh. This often includes rhythmic breathing patterns that align with sacred chanting, resulting in altered states of consciousness. One established practice is Kavvanah, in which breath is intentionally controlled to enhance focus on divine names or scriptures. This method can lead to a deep mystical absorption where everything fades away, leaving only the presence of Divinity.

Monks who practice Hesychasm employ slow, deep breathing techniques. They inhale while mentally reciting "Lord Jesus Christ, Son of God" and exhale while saying, "have mercy on me." This rhythmic breath work eventually leads to a state of deep inner silence, known as Hesychia. It can cause visions, experiences of divine light, and feelings of unity with God.

In Western Christianity, contemplative prayer uses breath as a tool to attain mystical awareness. The 14th-century text, The Cloud of Unknowing, outlines a breath-focused technique where one releases all thoughts and focuses solely on a sacred word or the presence of God. Breath serves as a means to eliminate distractions, enabling the individual to enter a state of pure, formless awareness.

PHYSIOLOGICAL AND PSYCHOLOGICAL EFFECTS OF MYSTICAL BREATH WORK

Modern neuroscience and psychology offer insights into how breath-centred mystical practices can lead to altered states. Controlled breathing activates the parasympathetic nervous system, reducing stress and promoting a sense of well-being. It also influences brainwave activity, transitioning from beta (normal consciousness) to alpha and theta waves associated with meditation and trance states. Prolonged breath-holding techniques like rapid breathing can induce hypoxia and heightened CO_2 levels, resulting in altered perceptions and mystical experiences. These physiological processes may clarify why mystics frequently describe radiant visions, divine interactions, and ego dissolution during deep prayer and meditation.

PRACTICAL APPLICATION: HOW TO INCORPORATE BREATH WORK INTO MYSTICAL PRACTICE

For those seeking to integrate breath-centred mysticism into their spiritual practice, the following methods can serve as a starting point: YHVH Breathing Meditation: Inhale on "Yod," hold on "Heh," exhale on "Vav," and pause on the final "Heh." This rhythmic cycle aligns breath with divine presence.

Jesus Prayer Breath work: Recite the Jesus Prayer mentally in sync with the breath, inhaling and exhaling in a slow, measured manner to enter deeper contemplation.

Rhythmic Chanting: Engage in Hasidic-style chanting with breath awareness, allowing melodies to guide the breath into ecstatic prayer states.

Silent Breath Awareness: Practice stillness with slow, deep breathing, letting each inhalation and exhalation draw attention inward toward divine presence.

Alternate Nostril Breathing: Inspired by monastic breath practices, alternate nostril breathing can help balance the nervous system before prayer or meditation.

Breath serves as a sacred channel to entangle with the divine in mysticism, enabling altered states of consciousness that enhance spiritual connection. Various techniques like YHVH breath meditation, ecstatic breathing, rhythmic Jesus Prayer, and silent breath awareness in contemplative prayer all highlight how the act of breathing can unveil mystical realms. In today's world full of distractions, revisiting the ancient practice of breath brings a way to find stillness, transformation, and encounters with Yahweh.

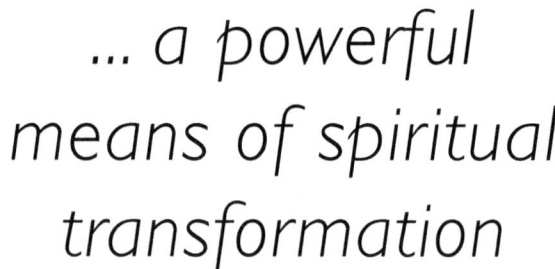

*... a powerful
means of spiritual
transformation*

Chanting: A Path to Higher Consciousness

Chanting has been a cornerstone of mystical practice for millennia, bridging the seen and unseen worlds through the power of vocalised sacred sound. Rooted in ancient religious traditions, chanting serves as a vehicle for spiritual ascent, transforming consciousness and connecting the practitioner to divine reality. Within mysticism, chanting functions as both a means of worship and a tool for achieving deeper states of awareness, unlocking the secrets of divine communion through vibrational resonance.

THE SCIENCE OF SOUND AND CONSCIOUSNESS

Mystics have known for centuries that sound vibrations impact consciousness. Recent advances in neuroscience have confirmed this idea, showing that rhythmic vocalisation can change brainwave patterns and help achieve meditative and trance-like states. Chanting can reduce internal chatter, balance brain activity, and induce profound relaxation, leading to a shifted perception of reality that can enhance mystical encounters.

THE HISTORICAL AND SCRIPTURAL FOUNDATIONS OF CHANTING

JEWISH MYSTICISM AND THE POWER OF SOUND

The practice of chanting in Jewish mystical traditions has its roots in biblical times. The Hebrew Bible highlights the significance of spoken and sung words, from the act of creation in Genesis ("And God said, 'Let there be light'") to the Psalms, which serve as poetic calls into the mystery. Through the recitation of sacred texts in the Temple of Jerusalem and the chanted prayers of the Levites, an ancient recognition of the spiritual power of sound is demonstrated. Mystic traditions, particularly during the medieval period, developed a more refined approach to chanting, emphasising the vibrational and numerical significance of Hebrew letters and words.

CHRISTIAN MYSTICISM AND THE CHANT TRADITION

Chant in Christian mysticism has its origins in the early liturgical traditions of the Church. The practice of psalmodic chanting in Jewish synagogues had a significant influence on early Christian worship, which eventually led to the creation of plainsong, the precursor to Gregorian chant. Church Fathers like Augustine and Ambrose acknowledged the transformative effect of sung prayer in purifying the soul and ascending the mind towards divine contemplation.

Monastic traditions, especially those of the Benedictines and Desert Fathers, have incorporated chanting as a crucial practice to attain Hesychia, a state of inner calmness and divine presence. The Jesus Prayer, frequently chanted rhythmically, is a key method in Eastern Orthodox mysticism. Hesychasts on Mount Athos practice this chanting style to synchronise breath, mind, and voice, ultimately leading to theosis or unity with God.

THE MECHANICS AND TECHNIQUES OF MYSTICAL CHANTING

TECHNIQUES OF JEWISH MYSTICAL CHANTING

Niggunim: Hasidic melodies sung repetitively without words to bypass intellectual constraints and induce divine ecstasy.

Divine Name Invocation: Chanting the sacred names of God (such as the Tetragrammaton or permutations of Adonai and Elohim) to align with divine energy.

Sephirotic Intonations: Meditative chanting based on the Kabbalistic Tree of Life, using divine emanations to access higher realms.

Tikkunim (Restorative Chanting): The Lurianic Kabbalists used vocalisation as part of Tikkun Olam, a practice of spiritual rectification and world repair.

TECHNIQUES OF CHRISTIAN MYSTICAL CHANTING

Gregorian and Byzantine Chant: Slow, melismatic chanting of scripture and prayers designed to elevate the worshipper's consciousness.

Jesus Prayer: Repetitive invocation of scripture often synchronised with breathing to enter a contemplative state.

Taizé Chants: Simple, meditative, and repetitive chants used in communal prayer to cultivate a spirit of contemplation.

Glossolalia (Speaking in Tongues): In Pentecostal and Charismatic Christian movements, spontaneous chanting and vocalisation serve as a means of divine communication.

The different names of God were spoken of earlier in the book.

THE ROLE OF CHANTING IN ACHIEVING HIGHER STATE OF CONSCIOUSNESS

MYSTICAL ECSTASY AND ONENESS IN GOD

Chanting is not merely a ritualistic practice but a powerful tool for attaining higher states of consciousness. In Jewish mysticism, particularly within the Hasidic tradition, chanting is a pathway to mystical fervour, where the individual loses awareness of self and merges with divinity. In Christian mysticism, chanting facilitates kenosis (self-emptying), for experiencing intensified presence of God.

THE TRANSFORMATIVE EFFECTS OF CHANTING

Altering Perception of Time and Space: Prolonged chanting creates a sense of timelessness, a hallmark of mystical experiences.

Spiritual Purification: Vibrations cleanse the soul, acting as a form of inner alchemy.

Divine Revelation: Many mystics report receiving visions, insights, or heightened intuition through chanting.

Healing and Wholeness: Sound has been understood as a medium for spiritual and even physical healing.

Chanting, deeply embedded in mystical traditions, remains a powerful means of spiritual transformation. The practice leads to profound states of consciousness, uniting the practitioner with God the divine. In an age where modern distractions cloud spiritual perception, the ancient art of chanting offers a timeless path to awakening, guiding mystics into the ineffable mystery of God's presence.

*... a revelation,
a beckoning, an
invitation.*

Sacred Geometry: The Divine Blueprint in Creation and Christian Mysticism

Einstein - "God does not play dice with the universe."

Sacred geometry is the language through which God manifests order, symmetry, and harmony in creation. It is the mathematical and spatial expression of God's wisdom, revealing the underlying structure of the cosmos. In Christian mysticism, sacred geometry is not just a philosophical or aesthetic principle but a reflection of divine intelligence, God's signature woven into the fabric of existence.

At the heart of sacred geometry lies the idea that certain patterns and proportions are not arbitrary but foundational to all life. These forms, like the Flower of Life, the Fibonacci sequence, the Vesica Piscis, and the Golden Ratio, govern everything from the arrangement of galaxies to the structure of a simple flower. The ancients recognised these patterns as sacred because they consistently appear in nature and resonate with the fundamental laws of the universe. In this way, sacred geometry provides an intersection between theology, metaphysics, and physics, unveiling how God's creation is rooted in mathematical precision.

THE LOGOS AND SACRED GEOMETRY

Christian theology speaks of the Logos, the divine Word, as the principle through which all things came into being (John 1:1-3). The Logos is more than a spoken word, it is the divine ordering intelligence behind creation. If God is the supreme architect, then sacred geometry is the blueprint through which divine order is established in the physical realm.

The Flower of Life, a geometric pattern composed of interlocking circles, is one of the most ancient symbols of creation. It represents the interconnectedness of all things and has been found in Christian sacred art, symbolising divine order. This pattern mirrors the unfolding of life and reflects how the Word of God continually sustains existence.

The Vesica Piscis, created by the meeting of two circles, is a sacred geometric shape with strong roots in Christian tradition. It symbolises Christ as the connection between heaven and earth, blending divinity, and humanity. This emblem is commonly featured in Christian art, like the representation of Christ in mandorlas, underscoring unity.

THE TEMPLE AND THE COSMOS

The ancient Israelites, following divine instruction, constructed the Tabernacle and later the Temple in Jerusalem according to specific geometric proportions (Exodus 25:9). These sacred spaces were designed in alignment with cosmic order, reflecting the heavenly sanctuary (Hebrews 8:5). Christian cathedrals, built under sacred geometric principles, are microcosms of the divine order—where light, space, and proportion lead the soul toward transcendence.

One of the most striking sacred geometrical principles used in these structures is the Golden Ratio (Phi), a proportion found in everything from the human body to the Parthenon and even the design of great cathedrals. This ratio, approximately 1.618, is often associated with divine beauty and perfection, demonstrating how physical creation mirrors the mathematical harmony of God's design.

Another divine principle seen in creation is the Fibonacci sequence, a numerical pattern that unfolds in a spiralling progression found in pinecones, galaxies, and even the human body. This sequence is often regarded as a fingerprint of God, showing the continuous unfolding of divine creation.

What the mystics have known in enraptured and vision, modern physics now glimpses the cosmos is not merely matter but vibration, rhythm and breath, a symphony of patterns inscribed by the unseen hand of the Creator.

At the quantum threshold, where the visible dissolves into mystery, energy moves in precise, harmonic structures, mirroring the sacred geometry that has long been etched into the fabric of creation. Subatomic particles flicker in and out of being, guided by unseen forces, tracing patterns of divine intention. The dance of wave functions, the curvature of spacetime, the spiralling arms of galaxies—all speak in the language of sacred form. The Fibonacci sequence unfurls in the spinning majesty of nebulae, just as it whispers through the petals of a rose and the curling tendrils of the sea's hidden shells. What is vast is also small, what is seen is also unseen, and all is held within the breath of divine wisdom.

Christian mysticism has always known this truth, not as knowledge but as revelation. Sacred geometry is the script of the Logos, the divine ordering Word that calls forth cosmos from chaos, light from darkness. It is the hidden language of God's wisdom, threading through all things, revealing the One who is before all, within all, and beyond all.

The Flower of Life, ancient and ineffable, speaks of creation's interwoven unity, a lattice of being where all life springs from the divine source. The Vesica Piscis, the sacred womb of light, holds the mystery of Christ, the intersection of heaven and earth, God, and man. The Golden Ratio, inscribed in beauty itself, is the measure of divine harmony, the blueprint of perfection found in the arc of a wave, the unfurling of a fern, the proportions of sacred temples. The Fibonacci sequence pulses through the heartbeat of creation, a golden thread weaving the seen and the unseen, the finite and the infinite.

This is no accident. This is no coincidence of nature. It is a revelation, a beckoning, an invitation. To explore sacred geometry unveils divine mysteries, revealing Christ's presence within creation's silent, geometric language. To look at these patterns is more than just seeing; it is beholding the meeting point of math and mysticism, where numbers intertwine and structure transforms into vision.

The universe is a cathedral, its pillars formed of sacred ratios, its vaults painted in spirals of stars. Every flower, every seashell, every whisper of wind across the waters sings the same silent hymn: the Word is here. The Word has been spoken, and it echoes in the fabric of reality. Let those with eyes to see, and those with ears hear. For the hidden geometry of creation is but the veil, thin and trembling, between the visible and the glory within.

... we are invited to participate in this eternal dance of relationship

Embracing Christian Mysticism in an Age of Scepticism, Doubt and Misinformation

In an age steeped in scepticism and disillusionment, many find themselves adrift, questioning the authenticity of spiritual experience.

True mysticism is no retreat into fantasy; it is a journey beyond the brittle limitations of tradition, a pilgrimage into the fathomless mystery of God. It is not an abandonment of reality but an immersion into its truest essence, a reality suffused with divine presence, shimmering in the unseen. Embarking on this mystical journey means entering the sacred, a realm where time intertwines with eternity, illuminating the finite through the Infinite. Without the mystic's vision, life becomes a wasteland of hollow pursuits, echoing with a quiet despair.

The great mystics have always recognised that divine union is achieved in the depths of the soul's darkest moments. St John of the Cross, in his Dark Night of the Soul, does not describe a gentle ascent but a passage through uncertainty, where the soul is rid of all illusions and stands exposed before Yahweh. This is not an escape from the world but a plunge into its profoundest layers, where divine love purges all that is false. To Embrace a mystical way of life comes with its sacrifices, yet the rewards surpass them greatly. Christian mysticism does not promote an isolated, self-centred awakening. It is no exclusive private ecstasy but a dissolving of the self into the greater whole, the Mystical Body of Christ, where love ceases to be a sentiment and becomes an all-consuming fire, a bliss drink of heightened ecstasy.

For those who criticise the historical shortcomings of institutional Christianity, its associations with performance, and its remnants of separation theology, mysticism doesn't aim to defend past mistakes. Instead, it urges for radical transformation and encourages embracing authenticity. It doesn't just recognise the injustices within religious institutions; it goes beyond them, urging believers to immerse themselves in the flames of divine love where all falsehood fades away. Christian mysticism stands in contrast to the scepticism of the era. It's not about being naïve but about possessing wisdom, not about avoiding reality, but about awakening to it. Choosing this path means delving into a reality that goes beyond surface appearances, where life itself unfolds as a journey in divine union.

LETTING GO

> "None of you can become my disciple if you do not give up all your possessions." — Luke 14:33

The initial threshold on the mystic path involves detachment, a profound letting go to create room for the authentic. It signifies releasing all that restricts the soul: mental constructs that aim to limit and control the Divine instead of allowing it to unfold from within.

Detachment is the letting go of identity that's framed in the old, and believe it or not, even the notion of God as we have known Him. No, we do not deny Jesus as Lord and saviour but tradition and institutional Christianity have taught a God that is rooted in a framework that contains and restricts His image rather than revealing Him. Meister Eckhart speaks of the necessity of emptying the heart: "No vessel can hold both wine and water. If a vessel is to contain wine, it must first be emptied of water." Similarly, the soul must rid itself of both the known falsehoods and the unknown ones.

Detachment is not about deprivation but liberation. It involves erasing false walls and dissolving illusions which can pertain to friendships, family, and more. The likelihood of losing family and friends is real, but letting go of what is not eternal, we are able to awaken to the One who truly is. The mystic path presents a paradox: by releasing everything, we ultimately gain everything.

THE TRANSFORMATIVE PROMISE OF DIVINE LOVE IN CHRISTIAN MYSTICISM

The core message of Christian mysticism is profoundly simple yet endlessly deep: God is love. This truth, deeply rooted in scripture, might seem unfathomable to many. How can we trust such an extravagant promise? Can the infinite Creator of the cosmos truly be intimately and passionately concerned with each of us? The idea of God's boundless, unconditional love may appear too idealistic. But mystics across the ages insist this love is not an abstract or distant concept, it is alive, personal, and transformational.

In the grand mystery of existence, Christian mystics see God not merely as an impersonal force or cosmic principle but as the source of conscious, radiant love. His love fuels the universe and is not aloof or detached; it seeks connection, intimacy, and union.

Mysticism asserts that God's love actively flows outward, touching and transforming every aspect of creation. This love does not merely sustain the universe; it seeks to dwell in the hearts of all who are willing to receive it. It is poured out with such generosity that no creature, no matter how seemingly insignificant, is beyond its embrace.

In this context, the mystics present a startling vision: God's love is not just something we receive passively; it is something we are invited to participate in. To be loved by God is to be transformed into love itself. This participation in divine love is at the heart of Christian mysticism. The invitation is not just to acknowledge God's love intellectually, but to live in it, to let it shape our hearts, and to become channels through which this love can flow to the world.

This transformative process is beautifully embodied in the Christian understanding of the Holy Trinity. For the mystics, the Trinity is not merely a theological concept but a lived reality of love in community. God is One, yet this unity encompasses three persons: the Father (Creator), the Son (Redeemer), and the Holy Spirit (Sustainer). This triune reality speaks of a divine love that is dynamic, relational, and endlessly self-giving. God is a communion of love, and we are invited to participate in this eternal dance of relationship.

Consider God the Creator, the source of all that exists. This is the God who, out of sheer love, brought the universe into being and continues to sustain it moment by moment. Creation itself is an expression of divine love, a masterpiece shaped by infinite wisdom and care. To contemplate the wonders of creation is to glimpse the beauty and generosity of the Creator's love.

Then there is God, the Redeemer, Jesus Christ, who embodies divine love in human form. In the life, death, and resurrection of Jesus, God's love is made tangible and accessible. Jesus walked among us, sharing in our struggles, joys, and sufferings. His message and example reveal that divine love is not abstract or remote but deeply personal. Jesus shows that God's love reaches out to the marginalised, the broken, and the lost. In his self-sacrificial love, we see the depth and cost of divine compassion. Jesus' resurrection, a victory over sin and death, affirms that God's love is not only redemptive but transformative, bringing new life and hope.

The Holy Spirit, the third person of the Trinity, is the active presence of divine love within us and among us. The Spirit is the comforter, the advocate, the one who empowers and unites. Through the Spirit, God's love takes root in our hearts, guiding and strengthening us. The Spirit binds us together as the body of Christ, a community of love called to reflect God's love for the world.

To receive this triune love is to be drawn into a way of living that reflects the very nature of God. Jesus summarised this way of life with a simple yet profound command: love God with all your heart, soul, mind, and strength, and love your neighbour as yourself (Mark 12:30–31). These three dimensions of love—love for God, love for others, and love for oneself—are inseparable. Just as the persons of the Trinity exist in a relationship of perfect unity, these expressions of love form a complete and harmonious whole.

Loving God means opening ourselves fully to His divine presence, surrendering to the infinite love that seeks to fill us. It is a posture of trust, gratitude, and adoration. This love calls us into a relationship of intimacy and communion with the One who is the source of all being.

Loving our neighbour flows naturally from loving God. The more we experience God's love, the more we are empowered to share that love with others. Our neighbours are not just those who are like us or those we find easy to love. In the expansive vision of Christian mysticism, our neighbours include the stranger, the outcast, and even our enemies. Divine love breaks down barriers, teaching us to see every person as a beloved child of God. To love our neighbour is to become instruments of God's healing, justice, and mercy in the world.

Loving ourselves is often the most challenging aspect. Yet Jesus' command to love our neighbours as ourselves implies that self-love is not selfish but essential. To love ourselves rightly is to recognise our worth as sons made in God's image and beloved by God. It is to accept ourselves with humility and grace, knowing we are works in progress, continually being shaped by divine love. True self-love is grounded in the understanding that we are not separate from God's love but are participants in it.

Christian mysticism reveals that divine love is fundamentally self-giving. Just as God pours love into us, we are called to pour out love to others. This giving and receiving of love is a reflection of the eternal exchange within the Trinity. The more we give ourselves in love, the more we are filled with love. In this way, love becomes a cycle of grace, a continuous flow that renews and transforms both the giver and the receiver.

When we allow ourselves to be transformed by divine love, we enter into what the mystics describe as a cosmic dance. This dance is one of joy, beauty, and communion. It is a dance that transcends time and space, drawing us into the eternal life of God. In this dance, we experience the fullness of being, the restoration of our true selves, and the healing of all brokenness.

The promise of Christian mysticism is astonishing: through divine love, we are invited to partake in the very life of God. This participation is not reserved for a select few but is open to all who will receive it. God's love is lavish, overflowing, and inexhaustible. It seeks to transform not only individuals but all of creation. As we are filled with divine love, we become agents of that love in the world, contributing to the healing and restoration of all things.

To be loved by God is to be drawn into a reality far greater than ourselves. It is to experience a love transcending all understanding yet is intimately present. In being loved, we become love. This is the heart of Christian mysticism: a call to be transformed, to embody divine love, and to join in the eternal dance of joy and communion that will one day encompass the entire cosmos.

THE HEART OF PILGRIMAGE

The concept of pilgrimage and the journey has held spiritual significance across mystical traditions. This theme is embedded in scripture, mystical literature, and the broader fabric of religious experience. It represents an inner transformation of the soul, unlocking a divine union. Pilgrimage is the ascent of the spirit and soul through stages of entanglement, enlightenment, and, ultimately, the mystical expression of unification with God.

ORIGINS OF PILGRIMAGE IN SCRIPTURE

The concept of pilgrimage can be traced back to ancient scriptural narratives that portray the journey as a sacred encounter, closely linked to the idea of the Promised Land in the Hebrew Bible. The Israelites' voyage from enslavement to freedom in the Exodus is considered the fundamental model of pilgrimage. Their expedition from Egypt to Mount Sinai and ultimately to the Land of Canaan is a voyage of belief and change, a transformation into destiny. In Exodus 19:4, God reminds Moses of the journey, saying, "You yourselves have seen what I did to Egypt, and how I carried you on eagles' wings and brought you to myself." This verse encapsulates the essence of pilgrimage as a journey toward the manifestation of Divine Presence.

In scripture, pilgrimage is showcased through Jesus' trip to Jerusalem for the Passover, which ends with his Passion. This journey is recounted in the Gospels, notably in Luke 9:51, where it mentions, "When the days drew near for him to be taken up, he set his face to go to Jerusalem." This reflects a profound spiritual significance. Jesus' physical pilgrimage symbolises his redemptive mission and the believer's spiritual journey towards salvation in Him.

THE MYSTICAL SIGNIFICANCE OF PILGRIMAGE

In mystical literature, pilgrimage is not merely a journey across landscapes but an unfolding of the soul's deepest longing for divine inheritance, a birthright concealed in the ineffable depths of Yahweh's heart. It is a movement of the heart, where each step reflects an inner transformation, a primordial echo in the corridors of eternity. The physical path dissolves into a spiritual ascent, a transformation that leads the mystic beyond the immediate into the luminous embrace of divine unity. In this sacred unfolding, time bends, space contracts, and the journey itself becomes the destination—an ever-deepening surrender into mystery.

> Pilgrimage, then, is not about reaching a place, it is a drawing inward, a response to the magnetic pull of the love of the Father into the realm of becoming.

In this sacred unfolding, the soul relinquishes its weight, casting off the garments of the known to step barefoot into the ineffable. The road is no longer a means but an initiation, a corridor of transformation where every breath becomes prayer, every step a sanctification. To embark upon pilgrimage is not to seek a distant threshold, it is to become the threshold itself, the living path where heaven and earth converge, where longing dissolves into union, and the journey and the destination are one. The mystical journey is one of transformation, where the mystic seeks to transcend the material world and behold the hidden face of Mystery.

In Christian mysticism, pilgrimage is not an end in itself but a means of divine encounter and self-transformation. The physical journey symbolises an interior ascent where one confronts obstacles, experiences revelations, and gradually unfolds a divine union, a position attained through the Cross of Jesus. Pilgrimage invites believers to see their lives as a sacred mystical journey, full of meaning, purpose, and the potential for mystical union.

A SPIRITUAL AWAKENING

Hebrew Roots of Awakening: עור ('ūr) and קום (qum)

In Hebrew tradition, two profound words capture the essence of spiritual awakening: עור ('ūr) and קום (qum). These terms go beyond mere wakefulness; they signify consciousness, action, and transformation.

The Prophet Isaiah calls out to Jerusalem: "Awake, awake, put on your strength, O Zion" (Isaiah 52:1).

This is more than a call to attention, it is an urgent summons to rise into divine identity. The repetition of עוּרִי (ʿūrī) intensifies the plea, urging a spiritual reawakening from lethargy. To put on strength is to clothe oneself in divine purpose, an awakening that is both personal and communal.

King David expresses a similar cry in Psalm 57:8: "Awake, my glory! Awake, harp and lyre!"

Here, עוּרָה (ʿūrāh) is directed inward, calling his kavod (glory), the innermost divine essence—to awaken. The imagery of the harp and lyre symbolises the soul aligning with the cosmic harmony of existence.

In the Song of Solomon 5:2, the mystical language of love and longing reveals a deeper truth: "I slept, but my heart was awake."

This paradox highlights the soul's condition: even when the body sleeps, the heart—the spiritual core—remains vigilant, ever ready for divine encounter. The soul listens for the gentle knocking of the Beloved, poised for divine communion.

Greek Perspectives: Ἔγειρε (egeire) and ἀνάστασις (anastasis)

In Greek mystical thought, ἔγειρε (egeire) and ἀνάστασις (anastasis) embody the idea of rising from ignorance into divine illumination.

The Apostle Paul echoes an ancient hymn of awakening in Ephesians 5:14: "Awake, O sleeper, and arise from the dead."

Here, ἔγειρε (egeire)—wake up—combines with ἀνάστα (anasta)—rise up. The sleeper is not just someone physically asleep but one spiritually dormant, trapped in material inertia. To arise from the dead is to be reborn into spiritual consciousness, illuminated by divine light.

Romans 13:11 reinforces this theme: "Now it is time for you to awaken from sleep."

The word ἐγερθῆναι (egerthēnai) implies more than waking—

it is a resurrection, a reorientation of the soul toward divine truth. ὕπνου **(hypnou)**—sleep—symbolises spiritual neglect. To awaken is to reclaim awareness of divine reality.

In Mark 5:41, Jesus calls to Jairus' daughter: "Little girl, I say to you, arise."

This simple command carries profound power. It is both a physical awakening and a symbol of the soul's ultimate resurrection, a return to life through divine grace.

Mystical Parallels: The Call from Above and Below

The Zohar explores awakening through the interplay of Itaruta de-Letata (arousal from below) and Itaruta de-Le'ela (arousal from above). In Zohar, we read:

"Awake, O north wind, and come, O south wind!"

This dual invocation reflects the interaction between human effort and divine grace. When the soul stirs to its divine potential, it draws down a cascade of celestial light.

Similarly, the Sefer Yetzirah states:

"Through the voice and the spirit, the heart is awakened."

In Kabbalistic thought, the heart is the seat of perception. To awaken it is to unlock the mysteries of creation, aligning oneself with the divine order.

Conclusion: The Path of Spiritual Awakening

The Hebrew עור ('ūr) and Greek ἔγειρε **(egeire)** form a bridge between two ancient mystical traditions. Whether in the prophet's urgent cry to Zion, the psalmist's plea to his soul, or the apostle's call to rise, the theme of awakening is universal and timeless.

Spiritual awakening moves us from forgetfulness to remembrance, from slumber to vigilance, from death to life. It is a quickening to return to our true essence, divine beings clothed in human experience. To awaken is to become conscious of the divine spark within, to rise in radiant awareness, reflecting the Infinite light.

As Ephesians 5:14 proclaims:

> "Awake, O sleeper, and arise from the dead, and Christ will shine on you."

May we heed this call, awakening to the mystery within and the mystical beyond, ever drawing us into the mystery of the infinite presence of Yahweh.

... love serves as the primary means of connection

Mystics that left a Legacy

JULIAN OF NORWICH

Julian of Norwich, a 14th-century English anchoress and mystic, holds a unique place in Christian spirituality for her deeply contemplative insights into the nature of God, suffering, and love. Living through the turbulence of the Black Death and the Peasants' Revolt, Julian's mystical revelations provided a radically hopeful vision in the face of despair. Her work, *Revelations of Divine Love*, is the earliest surviving book in English authored by a woman. More significantly, it offers an enduring spiritual message grounded in trust, compassion, and an unwavering belief in divine love, making her an essential figure in the history of Christian mysticism.

A Life Rooted in Contemplation

Julian of Norwich's life remains somewhat shrouded in mystery, a quality befitting her mystical vocation. Born around 1342, she chose the life of an anchoress—a solitary form of devotion in which she lived in a small cell attached to St. Julian's Church in Norwich. From this quiet sanctuary, Julian's life became one of prayer, reflection, and spiritual counsel. Her desire for isolation was not a retreat from the world but a deeper engagement with the mysteries of faith. It was within these humble confines that Julian received the visions, which would later be recorded as *Revelations of Divine Love*.

Revelations of Divine Love

In 1373, at the age of thirty, Julian suffered a grave illness, believed to be fatal. During this period of extreme physical weakness, she experienced a series of sixteen mystical visions or "showings" in which she saw profound images of Christ's Passion, the Blessed Virgin Mary, and the nature of God's love. After recovering, Julian spent years contemplating and interpreting these visions, eventually producing both a 'Short Text' and a more developed 'Long Text' of her experiences.

Central to Julian's theology is her emphasis on God's unconditional love and the assurance that, in the fullness of divine providence, "all shall be well." This message of ultimate hope and reconciliation stands out against the backdrop of a medieval society, often preoccupied with sin, judgment, and suffering. Julian's writings depart from many of the harsher doctrines of her time. Instead of emphasising wrath and punishment, she perceives God as pure, boundless love. Her vision of God's relationship with humanity is maternal, nurturing, and intimate. One of her most famous affirmations is:

"All shall be well, and all shall be well, and all manner of things shall be well." (Revelations of Divine Love, Chapter 27)

This declaration reflects a profound theological belief held by Julian. She believed that even the concept of sin is encompassed within God's providential design. The eternal love of God guarantees that, despite the world's darkness and suffering, divine goodness will prevail. This unwavering hope has brought comfort to many, especially in times of crisis. Julian presented a groundbreaking perspective on sin and redemption. Unlike other theologians of her era, who viewed sin as a cause for hopelessness, Julian saw it as an opportunity to deepen one's understanding of God's mercy. This notion implies while sin is present and should be acknowledged, it is part of a larger divine scheme that ultimately leads to redemption and a closer relationship with God. In her visions, Julian perceived God not as a harsh judge but as a perpetually compassionate and empathetic presence. This compassionate view of sin represents a significant departure from the prevailing theology of her time, which emphasised fear and punishment.

The Motherhood of God

One of Julian's most striking contributions to Christian mysticism is her depiction of God in maternal terms. While traditional Christian theology typically refers to God in paternal language, Julian offers a refreshing and deeply personal understanding of God as Mother. She describes Christ as nurturing humanity with the same tender care that a mother shows to her child. This maternal imagery underscores God's intimacy, gentleness, and sacrificial love.

Julian writes: "As truly as God is our Father, so truly is God our Mother." (Revelations of Divine Love, Chapter 59)

This theological insight opens up a profound avenue for understanding the multiplicity of God's nature. Julian's maternal language challenges rigid gender constructs and emphasises the all-encompassing, nurturing aspect of Yahweh. Her vision allows for a deeper, more holistic relationship with God, one that embraces both strength and tenderness, justice and mercy.

Julian's Impact on Mysticism and Beyond

Julian's impact on mysticism is seen not only in her unique

theological perspectives but also in her lasting relevance. Her writings have inspired theologians, spiritual seekers, and contemplatives for generations. Her message of divine love and hope resonates through time and different traditions, presenting an alternative to fear-based spirituality. Modern readers discover in Julian's work a voice that addresses universal human experiences such as suffering, doubt, and the desire for divine assurance. Her visions of a loving God have influenced prominent figures like Thomas Merton, Evelyn Underhill, and many contemporary mystics who aim to blend faith with a compassionate view of humanity. Her emphasis on the inherent goodness of creation and the eventual reconciliation of all things with God presents mysticism firmly grounded in hope and affirmation.

Julian of Norwich's mystical writings serve as a testament to the transformative power of divine love. Her visions, received during a time of personal and societal suffering, present a vision of God's unconditional, all-encompassing grace. Amid uncertainty and despair, her words remind us that love is the universe's foundation, and that ultimately, "all shall be well." Julian's deep trust in God's providence still inspires a spirituality of resilience, compassion, and unwavering hope. In a world grappling with suffering and complexity, her voice resonates, encouraging us to view the world through the perspective of divine love—a love that heals, nurtures, and ultimately redeems all things.

ST FRANCIS OF ASSISI

St. Francis of Assisi (1181/82–1226) remains one of the most transformative figures in the Christian mystical tradition, an embodiment of radical humility, poverty, and a living testament to a theology of deep, experiential union with God. His life, teachings, and mystical insights continue to ripple across centuries, offering profound pathways for those seeking intimacy with God and a renewed understanding of humanity's relationship with creation.

Born Giovanni di Pietro di Bernardone in the Umbrian town of Assisi, Francis grew up surrounded by the privileges of merchant-class life. However, his heart began to long for a different kind of richness - the wealth of spiritual poverty and unity with God. His mystical path did not originate in scholarly or theological study but in a direct experience of the Divine through nature, poverty, and deep love for all living beings. At the core of his mysticism was the belief that God could be seen in every aspect of creation, inspiring him to adopt a lifestyle of simplicity and fraternity with every creature. With no worldly possessions, Francis mystically discovered that he was filled with the boundless richness of God's love.

This radical poverty was also an act of mystical imitation of Christ. By seeking to become poor, Francis mirrored the humility of the Incarnation, the Word made flesh in utter vulnerability. His example became a living reminder that God meets humanity most intimately in weakness and humility. As he once said, "I have been all things unholy. If God can work through me, He can work through anyone." This profound humility cultivated a mystical openness. By relinquishing all claims to status, power, or entitlement, Francis created space for God to act freely through him. His life thus became a vessel for divine light, a transparency through which others could see the radiance of God.

Nature and the Cosmic Mysticism of St. Francis

Francis made a significant contribution to mysticism through his deep connection with the natural world. He viewed creation not just as a backdrop to human life but as a sacred and living manifestation of God's presence. His renowned work, the "Canticle of the Sun," beautifully captures this mystical perspective. In the canticle, he praises God through references to elements of nature like "Brother Sun," "Sister Moon," and even "Sister Death," seeing everything in the universe as part of a divine family created by God. This way of perceiving the world goes beyond a utilitarian or human-centred view of nature. Francis embraced a sacramental worldview where each aspect of creation reflected the beauty and love of God. His mysticism was all-encompassing, connecting him in a sacred bond with all creation. His profound sense of unity with nature foreshadowed later theological ideas, such as Teilhard de Chardin's ecological spirituality and modern ecotheology movements. Francis' teachings emphasise the importance of showing compassion and empathy to all of God's creatures, as he believed that a disconnect from nature inevitably leads to a disconnect from our fellow human beings and from God. In his mystical consciousness, love was indivisible — to love God authentically required love for all of creation.

The Stigmata and Mystical Union

One of the most significant events in Francis' life, showcasing the depth of his mystical connection with Christ, took place in the year 1224 on Mount La Verna. Engaged in a 40-day retreat of fasting and prayer, Francis saw a vision of seraphim with the crucified Christ at its core. As the vision concluded, Francis bore the stigmata, wounds resembling those of Christ's crucifixion. The stigmata transcended mere physicality; it represented Francis' profound mystical unity with Christ's compassionate love. By carrying these wounds, Francis not only shared in Christ's suffering but also in His redeeming love for humanity. This mystical connection surpassed any imitation, growing into a deep engagement with the divine essence of sacrificial love. Francis' encounter with the stigmata served as an inspiration for future mystics to pursue a transformative union with God, moving beyond mere intellectual or emotional connections. His mystical journey was not about avoiding suffering but rather embracing it - recognising God's presence most profoundly in vulnerability and selfless love.

Influence on Mysticism and Beyond

Francis had a significant impact on Christian mysticism, with the Franciscan order he established serving as a fertile ground for mystical theology. This influenced figures like St. Bonaventure, who merged Francis' intuitive, nature-based mysticism with scholastic thought. Subsequently, mystics such as St. Clare of Assisi, St. John of the Cross, and St. Teresa of Avila continued the Franciscan focus on humility, and the soul's journey towards union with God. Francis' mystical insights extended beyond Christianity, as seen in his respectful encounter with Sultan al-Kamil during the Fifth Crusade. This encounter showcased his deep appreciation for mystical aspects of other faith traditions. His openness and humility set the stage for inter-religious dialogue rooted in shared spiritual experiences rather than doctrinal disputes.

The Call of St. Francis for Modern Mystics

In an era characterised by ecological crisis, excessive consumerism, and spiritual disconnection, the mysticism of St. Francis holds a profound significance. His message of embracing simplicity, universal love, and recognising God in all of creation provides a timeless remedy to the disarray of contemporary life. St. Francis emphasises that mysticism is not a secretive pursuit but a revolutionary way of life where every moment, every being, and every breath unveils divine love. In essence, St. Francis of Assisi's mystical heritage serves as a guiding light of transformative love, humility, and interconnectedness. His life exemplifies not only teachings but a tangible demonstration of being open to God's presence. His impactful words and revolutionary deeds continue to inspire us to adopt a mysticism that is wholly embodied, deeply humble, and fully attuned to the marvels of God's creation.

ST. THERESA OF AVILA

Saint Teresa of Ávila (1515–1582), also known as Teresa of Jesus, holds a unique position in Christian mysticism history. She was a Carmelite nun, reformer, writer, and visionary who not only revived the spiritual practices of her era but also established a mystical theology legacy influencing contemplative spirituality. Her notable works, like 'The Interior Castle' and 'The Way of Perfection', offer profound insights into the soul's journey toward divine union. Her teachings stress the importance of inner transformation through prayer, discipline, and divine grace. In a period dominated by religious reform, political turmoil, and ecclesiastical strictness in Europe, Teresa's voice stood out as a guide to direct experiential knowledge of God.

Mysticism in the Life of Teresa

Teresa of Ávila's mysticism was characterised by her personal encounters with the divine, which were deeply experiential. Her mystical experiences included visions, ecstasies, and moments of profound union with God, often accompanied by physical manifestations. One well-known incident was the 'transverberation of her heart', where she described an angel piercing her heart with a golden lance, symbolising the soul's complete surrender to divine love. These encounters did not disconnect her from the world; instead, they empowered her to engage more deeply with human experiences and with her efforts to reform the Carmelite order.

Teresa's approach to mysticism was grounded in practicality and intertwined with daily life, rather than being escapist or ethereal. She believed that the mystical journey was intimately linked with earthly responsibilities leading to their transformation. In her work 'The Interior Castle', she outlined a path for the soul's progression through seven "mansions" towards the innermost chamber where God dwells. This journey, she explained, involves a gradual release of ego, false attachments, and self-will, culminating in the soul's union with Yahweh.

One of Teresa's most well-known and profound statements captures the balance between active and contemplative life:

"God walks among the pots and pans."

This simple yet profound statement embodies her belief that God is always present, even in the most ordinary moments. To Teresa, the kitchen, with all its noise and busyness, is just as sacred as a chapel. She viewed the mystical journey not as a way to escape from the world but as a means to sanctify it by recognising God's constant presence.

Teresa's Vision of Prayer

Prayer, for Teresa, was the gateway to mystical union. She distinguished between various stages of prayer, ranging from vocal prayer to the highest forms of contemplative absorption. In her famous work 'The Way of Perfection', she provided practical guidance for her fellow sisters on how to cultivate a life of prayer. For Teresa, prayer was not merely a mental exercise or a recitation of formulas; it was a loving dialogue with God, a "conversation between friends."

Her insistence on prayer as a relational and transformative process is encapsulated in another of her profound statements:

"Let nothing disturb you, let nothing frighten you. All things pass away; God never changes. Patience obtains all things. Whoever has God lacks nothing; God alone suffices."

The quote is taken from her poem 'Nada te turbe' and emphasises the core of her mystical teachings. In a world marked by uncertainty and chaos, Teresa's wisdom guides the soul towards the unchanging truth of God. Her mystical approach involved deep trust and surrender, representing a bold release of fear and anxiety in favour of embracing the comforting essence of divine love.

The Reform of the Carmelites and the Legacy of Her Mystici

Teresa had a significant impact on Christian mysticism that extended beyond her personal spiritual experiences and writings. She reformed the Carmelite order, creating the Discalced Carmelites, to reflect her mystical insights on the importance of simplicity, humility, and true devotion. Observing a lack of discipline and focus in existing religious communities, Teresa founded convents where a strict commitment to poverty, prayer, and contemplation was central to communal life. Despite facing opposition, scepticism, ridicule, and persecution from religious authorities, she remained steadfast in her mission, driven by a deep sense of purpose. Teresa's reforms set the stage for a spiritual revival that not only influenced her followers but also shaped the practices of mystics and contemplatives for generations to come.

Teresa's mystical teachings placed a strong emphasis on the presence of God within the soul. In contrast to some mystical beliefs that highlight the separation between man and God, Teresa stressed the close proximity of God. In her work 'The Interior

Castle', she depicted the soul as a crystal-like fortress where God lives at the core, eagerly anticipating the soul's inward journey. This journey, according to her, demands bravery, self-awareness, and divine assistance. Teresa regarded self-awareness as a crucial aspect of mysticism. She believed that humility and understanding oneself were essential for achieving unity with God. Her famous quote, "Humility is truth," served as a reminder to her followers that recognising one's limitations and strengths is fundamental to spiritual growth.

Teresa's Influence on Mysticism and Beyond

The influence of Teresa of Ávila on Christian mysticism is profound and enduring. She was canonised in 1622 and proclaimed a Doctor of the Church in 1970, becoming the first woman to receive this honour. Her teachings continue to inspire theologians, mystics, and laypeople across different Christian denominations. Her writings are not only revered within Catholicism but also widely studied by Protestant and Orthodox Christians, as well as scholars of comparative religion. Teresa's impact can be observed in the works of later mystics like St. John of the Cross, her spiritual partner, and contemporary figures such as Thomas Merton and Mother Teresa of Calcutta, who drew inspiration from her profound spiritual insights. Her deep psychological understanding, particularly of the complexities of the human soul, foreshadows modern contemplative practices and psychological therapies. In an era characterised by spiritual exploration, Teresa's message of achieving intimate union with God through prayer, humility, and active love remains as pertinent as ever. She effectively bridges the gap between the mystical and the ordinary, demonstrating that the sublime experience of divine contemplation is accessible even amid daily life.

Ultimately, Teresa of Ávila's mysticism serves as a testament to the powerful transformation brought about by divine love. Her life and writings show that the mystical journey is not exclusive to a select few but is a calling for all those who yearn to explore the profound presence of God. Through her experiences, she extends an invitation for us to embark on our personal inner pilgrimage - a voyage that guides us towards the core of God. As she reassures us, it is in this sacred place that "God alone suffices."

ST. MECHTHILD OF MAGDEBURG

Mechthild of Magdeburg (c. 1207–c. 1282/1294) is a prominent figure in Christian mysticism. Coming from the medieval German world, she was a Beguine and visionary whose life and writings made a significant impact on the theological landscape of the 13th century. Her major work, 'The Flowing Light of the Godhead' (Das fließende Licht der Gottheit), is considered one of the most important mystical works in Christian history. It combines poetry, ecstatic visions, and a deep connection with God, offering both criticism and celebration. Mechthild's radical encounters with God and her courageous writings greatly influenced mysticism, influencing future mystics and reformers.

The Life of Mechthild

Born into a noble family near Magdeburg, Mechthild claimed to have received her first divine visions at the age of twelve. At around twenty, she left the comforts of aristocratic life to join the Beguine movement in Magdeburg. The Beguines, a semi-monastic community of women devoted to piety and service, offered Mechthild the freedom to pursue her spiritual calling without the constraints of formal religious orders. Profound interiority and outward boldness marked Mechthild's life. She described her mystical experiences with startling immediacy, giving voice to her intimate union with God while fearlessly critiquing the Church's corruption and worldliness. In her later years, she joined the Cistercian nuns at the convent of Helfta, where she found refuge and fellowship among other visionary women such as Gertrude of Helfta and Mechthild of Hackeborn.

The Flowing Light of the Godhead

Mechthild's primary work, 'Das fließende Licht der Gottheit,' was written in Middle Low German, a departure from the norm during a period when theological texts were mostly in Latin. By opting for the vernacular language, Mechthild sought to make her visions and teachings more accessible to a wider audience, particularly women and laypeople. Comprising seven books, her work seamlessly blends lyrical poetry, allegory, and direct dialogues with God, offering a vivid depiction of divine love. At the core of 'The Flowing Light' lies Mechthild's vision of God as the Beloved - a deity characterised by intense love, with a presence that is both ecstatic and fiery. Her mysticism captures a vibrant interplay between human desires and divine fulfilment, showcasing a profound exchange of love.

One of her most famous and profound statements encapsulates this intense relationship with Jesus:

"I cannot dance, Lord, unless You lead me. If You want me to leap joyfully, You must first show me how to dance and sing."

This passage beautifully illustrates her understanding of the soul's movement toward God as a divine dance. In Mechthild's vision, the soul's desire for God is met with an equally ardent desire on God's part to be united with the soul. This dance of mutual love signifies the mystic's life as one of surrender, responsiveness, and intimate joy.

Mystical Themes in Mechthild's Work

Mechthild's mysticism is characterised by several key themes: the centrality of love, the experience of divine light, and the call for reform. Her visions often portray God as a consuming fire of love that purifies and transforms the soul. This divine love is not abstract but deeply personal and experiential, requiring the mystic to risk everything for the sake of union with God. In her writings, light serves as a powerful metaphor for divine presence. According to Mechthild, God's love flows like light, illuminating, healing, and guiding the soul. The soul, in return, becomes a vessel of this light, reflecting God's radiance back into the world.

Another profound quote from 'The Flowing Light of the Godhead' reflects this theme of divine illumination:

"The soul is made of love, and must ever strive to return

to love. Therefore, it can never find rest nor happiness in other things. It must lose itself in love."

Here, Mechthild affirms that the essence of the soul is love, and its ultimate goal is to return to the origin of that love, which is God. This continuous pursuit, characterised by "losing oneself" in love, serves as the mystic's route to transformation. The soul's voyage involves not only seeking God but also merging with God, a profound act of complete surrender and selflessness.

Mechthild's Critique of the Church

Mechthild went beyond describing mystical union with her boldness. She fearlessly criticised the ecclesiastical structures of her time, as her visions often showed God's disapproval of clerical corruption, spiritual apathy, and the neglect of the poor. Despite facing significant opposition and accusations of heresy, Mechthild courageously confronted these issues due to her firm belief in divine love triumphing over human institutions. Her critiques were not rebellious but driven by a deep longing to witness the Church embodying God's love and justice. In doing so, she foreshadowed the reformist mindset of later figures such as Meister Eckhart and the Rhineland mystics.

Influence on Mysticism

Mechthild had a significant impact on Christian mysticism. Her writings influenced her contemporaries and future generations, such as John Tauler, Henry Suso, and even the great reformer Martin Luther, who appreciated her directness and theological depth. Her mystical insights laid the groundwork for bridal mysticism, which depicts the soul's union with God as a spiritual marriage. Additionally, by choosing to write in the vernacular, Mechthild helped democratise mystical theology. By sharing her visions in a way that was understandable to everyone, she empowered ordinary people, especially women, to explore and express their own connections with God. This emphasis on personal experience and direct encounters with Yahweh would resonate throughout the later mystical traditions of Europe.

Mechthild of Magdeburg is celebrated as a symbol of mystical courage and divine love. Her life and writings serve as a powerful reminder that the mystical journey involves a deep connection with God and bold interaction with the world. Her spiritual union with Christ inspires us to immerse ourselves in love and allow it to shine throughout our existence. Mechthild's visions, poetry, and unwavering dedication to truth establish her as a significant figure in Christian mysticism. Her words, akin to the light she frequently depicted, continue to enlighten, change, and guide us toward God's essence.

THE CLOUD OF UNKNOWING

The 'Cloud of Unknowing' stands as one of the most compelling and enigmatic works of Christian mysticism, composed in the latter half of the 14th century by an anonymous English author. This anonymous writer, traditionally referred to as the 'Cloud-author', offered an enduring vision of the soul's journey toward union with God through a process of loving surrender and unknowing. This work profoundly shaped mystical thought, impacting numerous theologians, contemplatives, and those seeking divine union for generations. Its legacy lies in the tension between the limitations of the intellect and the boundless depths of divine mystery—a tension that the 'Cloud-author' so skilfully delineates.

Historical and Theological Context

The 'Cloud of Unknowing' emerged during a period of significant upheaval in medieval Europe. The 14th century bore witness to the Black Death, socio-political instability, and a Church struggling to maintain spiritual authority. Against this backdrop, a deep hunger for authentic spiritual experience and a more intimate relationship with God took root. The work reflects the thriving mystical tradition in England at the time, connected to the writings of figures such as Julian of Norwich, Walter Hilton, and Richard Rolle.

The 'Cloud-author' speaks directly to a world grappling with uncertainty, offering a radical approach to divine encounter: one that emphasises humility, contemplation, and the relinquishment of human reasoning in the face of God's ineffable nature. The text was likely intended as a guide for a young disciple exploring contemplative prayer, but its insights transcend its immediate context, addressing all who seek a deeper union.

The Path of Unknowing

At the core of the 'Cloud of Unknowing' is a paradox: understanding God comes through unknowing. This doesn't mean disregarding reason but intentionally letting go of the mind's constraints to connect with God through love. The author emphasises that true understanding of God is achieved by releasing all preconceptions and complexities. Rather than holding onto specific notions of God, individuals should enter a realm of unknowing, a holy realm beyond intellectual grasp.

"For He may well be loved but not thought. By love He may be gotten and held, but by thought never."

This passage discusses a fundamental principle of apophatic (negative) theology, which suggests that God surpasses human comprehension and categories. The intellect, while valuable, can hinder understanding when it tries to confine the boundless within limited concepts. Therefore, in the "cloud of unknowing," you step into a darkness that is not despairing but filled with divine mystery, where love serves as the primary means of connection. The Importance of Humility and Love The author of "The Cloud" underscores the significance of humility in the contemplative journey. The process of unknowing does not involve gaining esoteric knowledge or reaching spiritual heights through personal striving; instead, it entails letting go of ego and pride. Through this release, the heart becomes receptive to God's indescribable presence.

"Look that nothing live in thy working mind but a naked intent stretching unto God, not clothed in any special thought of God in thyself, how He is in Himself, or in any of His works, but only that He is as He is."

In this passage, the author emphasises the importance of having a clear and pure intention, devoid of any distractions or personal perceptions of God. The mystic is encouraged to uphold this sincerity like a constant flame shining in the darkness. The Cloud-author presents a type of prayer that transcends language, thoughts, and feelings, focusing instead on a state of complete attention and surrender.

Influence on Mysticism

The Cloud of Unknowing has had a profound and far-reaching impact on the mystical tradition. It influenced the development of contemplative prayer practices and resonated in later mystical writings, such as those of St. Teresa of Ávila and St. John of the Cross, Spanish Carmelites. The concept of the 'dark night of the soul' by St. John of the Cross shares similarities with the cloud of unknowing, both expressing the idea that encountering the divine often involves a journey through obscurity and surrender. Furthermore, the 'Cloud of Unknowing' foreshadowed certain themes in modern existential and phenomenological thought. The notion that a true divine encounter requires moving beyond the bounds of reason can be seen in the works of philosophers like Søren Kierkegaard and Martin Heidegger, who explored the limits of human cognition and the essence of being.

The 'Cloud-author' also had a significant impact on the Centering Prayer movement in the 20th century, especially through figures like Thomas Keating. Centering Prayer, a form of silent, contemplative prayer, closely aligns with the 'Cloud-author's' emphasis on letting go of thoughts and fostering a loving, wordless focus on God.

Feminine and Anonymous Voice

It is important to note the ambiguity of the Cloud-author's identity. Though traditionally presumed to be a male cleric, there is no definitive evidence regarding gender. The anonymity itself reflects the author's theological stance, that the self must vanish in the encounter with God. This namelessness, this erasure of ego, underscores the central theme of self-emptying. If we consider the possibility of a female author, we connect to a tradition of female mystics who embraced similar themes of divine intimacy through unknowing, such as Julian of Norwich. In either case, the anonymity of the Cloud-author allows the voice to transcend individual identity, offering a timeless guide regardless of era, gender, or circumstance.

The Cloud of Unknowing continues to shine as a light for those intrigued by profound mysteries. Its core message, emphasising the pursuit of God through love and embracing the unknown, challenges contemporary perspectives on knowledge, faith, and spirituality. Encouraging a release of the intellect and a deepening of the heart's intentions, The Cloud's author urges us to connect with God, not as an entity to comprehend but as a Presence to adore unconditionally. In a world that craves certainty, The Cloud of Unknowing presents a revolutionary and unconventional path: one characterised by humility, enigma, and love. This mystical realm, for those who dare enter, reveals not despair but a profound, loving closeness where all other knowledge yields.

... God is grasped not by thought but by love

The Endless Horizon of Divine Union as a Mystic

Christian mysticism is not merely a path; it is an invitation—a beckoning into the very heart of God. From the prophets of old to the contemplatives of the present, this sacred journey has been one of unveiling and surrender, an awakening to the hidden realities of primordial existence. The mystic's path is not an escape from the world but a deeper immersion into it, revealing that God is not distant but intimately interwoven with every breath, every moment, and every atom of creation.

As we have explored throughout this work, mysticism is not a relic of the past nor a niche within Christian thought—it is the very foundation upon which the spiritual life is built. The burning bush of Moses, the ecstatic visions of Ezekiel, the transfiguration of Christ, the divine indwelling proclaimed by Paul—these are not isolated events but signposts pointing to the eternal truth that Jesus is both beyond and within. To be a mystic is not to transcend the world but to see it anew, to recognise the divine signature written into the fabric of all things.

Mysticism is a journey of ascent, an ever-deepening movement toward divine union. And yet, it is also a descent—a surrender into the unknowing, a relinquishing of the need to grasp, control, or define the Infinite. The mystic stands at the threshold of paradox, where light and darkness converge, where knowledge and mystery intertwine, where presence and absence become one. To embrace this paradox is to step into the luminous darkness where God is known not through certainty but through love.

The call of the mystic is the call of Christ: "Abide in me, and I in you." This is the heart of all mystical experiences, a radical intimacy, a deep abiding in the divine presence that transforms everything it touches. To abide in Christ is to awaken to the truth that has always been, His presence is not found in some distant heaven but in the very core of our being. The veil has been torn; the Holy of Holies is now within.

Throughout history, mystics have sought to express this ineffable truth through language, symbol, and silence. The Cloud of Unknowing teaches God is grasped not by thought but by love. Meister Eckhart reminds us that to know God truly, we must become nothing so that God may be all. Julian of Norwich assures us that in the divine embrace, "All shall be well, and all manner of things shall be well." These voices, though separated by time and tradition, speak in harmony, whispering the same eternal truth: Love is the foundation of all things, and in love, all things return to God.

The mystical journey is filled with ecstasy, for it calls for the surrender of self, the emptying of the ego, the willingness to step beyond the known into the infinite unknown. The dark night of the soul is not a punishment but an unfolding, a purification that prepares the soul for the unmediated encounter with divine love. To walk the mystical path is to walk through fire, yet on the other side of the flame is a love so vast, so radiant, that nothing else remains.

So what now? What does one do with such knowledge? Mysticism is not an end but a beginning. It is not a doctrine to be learned but a life to be lived. It is the invitation to see the world as it truly is, saturated with divinity, shimmering with grace. The mystic sees Christ not only in the sanctuary but in the streets, not only in scripture but in the silence, not only in moments of rapture but in the everyday rhythms of daily life. There is no separation. There never was.

This is the final paradox, the great revelation: the journey never ends. And so, to those who hunger for the deep mysteries who have journeyed through these pages, your path is just beginning. The divine invitation stands before you. Step beyond words. Step beyond knowing. Step into the eternal embrace where all is made new. The mystery remains, yet it is here, in the heart of the unknown, that you will ascend and entangle your primordial existence in Christ as a New Creation being.

"The deeper we entangle into Yahweh, the further the horizon of mysticism extends, an endless unfolding into the mystery of divine love."

Resources

1. Origen (c. 185–c. 253 AD) Commentary on the Song of Songs*: In this work, Origen delves into the allegorical interpretation of the Song of Songs, emphasising the soul's mystical union with Christ. For insights into his views on divine mysteries and transformation through union with Christ, see pages 81–85.

2. Augustine of Hippo (354–430 AD) Confessions: Augustine reflects on his spiritual journey and mystical experiences. His interpretation of Paul's writings, especially regarding the inner transformation and vision of God, can be found in Book VII, Chapters 10–17. City of God: In Book X, Augustine discusses the nature of true worship and the soul's ascent to God, referencing Paul's emphasis on the indwelling Spirit.

3. Bernard of Clairvaux (1090–1153) Sermons on the Song of Songs: Bernard's sermons explore the intimate relationship between the soul and God, drawing on Pauline themes. For his reflections on the "face-to-face" encounter with God, see Sermon 31, particularly pages 131–135.

4. Meister Eckhart (c. 1260–c. 1328): Sermons: Eckhart's sermons often reference Paul's notion of self-transcendence and union with Christ. For example, in Sermon 52, he discusses the concept of becoming a "new person" in Christ, aligning with Galatians 2:20.

5. Julian of Norwich (c. 1342–c. 1416): Revelations of Divine Love: Julian reflects on the mystical indwelling of Christ within the soul. Her meditation on Paul's teachings about Christ's presence can be found in Chapter 54, pages 218–220.

6. Albert Schweitzer (1875–1965): The Mysticism of Paul the Apostle (1930): Schweitzer argues that Paul's theology centres on a mystical union with Christ. This is extensively discussed in Chapter 3, pages 68–102.

7. E.P. Sanders (1937–2020) Paul and Palestinian Judaism (1977): Sanders examines Paul's concept of participation in Christ. Relevant discussions are in Chapter 4, pages 432–437.

8. N.T. Wright (b. 1948): Paul and the Faithfulness of God (2013): Wright explores the mystical dimensions of Paul's theology. See Volume 2, Part III, Chapter 9, pages 805–812.

9. Gershom Scholem (1897–1982): Major Trends in Jewish Mysticism (1941): Scholem briefly mentions Paul in the context of Jewish mystical traditions. This is discussed in Lecture II, pages 52–54.

10. Daniel Boyarin (b. 1946): A Radical Jew: Paul and the Politics of Identity (1994): Boyarin examines Paul's mystical tendencies. See Chapter 2, pages 25–30.

11. Carl McColman's writings, particularly his book "The New Big Book of Christian Mysticism: The Essential Guide to Contemplative Spirituality."

12. Louis Bouyer's "Mysticism: An Essay on the History of the Word"

13. Pseudo-Dionysius the Areopagite's "The Mystical Theology"

14. John R. Mabry "Growing into God, A Beginners Guide to Christian Mysticism

15. Aryeh Kaplan – Meditation and Kabbalah. Rabbi Yitzchak Ginsburgh – Living in Divine Space and The Hebrew Letters.

16. Open Mind, Open Heart by Thomas Keating – Centering Prayer and contemplative engagement

17. Peter Brown – The Rise of Western Christendom.

18. Bart D. Ehrman – Lost Christianities and The Orthodox Corruption of Scripture.

19. Bruce Metzger – The Canon of the New Testament: Its Origin, Development, and Significance.

20. Quantum Enigma: Physics Encounters Consciousness, Bruce Rosenblum and Fred Kuttner.

21. Jewish Meditation: A Practical Guide, Aryeh Kaplan

22. Inner Space, Rabbi Aryeh Kaplan.

23. Centering Prayer and Inner Awakening, Cynthia Bourgeault

24. Breath of Life, Ron DelBene (on contemplative breathing prayer)

About the Author

Based in South Africa, I serve alongside my wife Bianca as the pioneering leader of 'Wells of Mem,' a dynamic Ekklesia in Midrand, Johannesburg. We're leading a mystic community that bridges the ancient ways with mystical spiritual practices, creating space for authentic transformation and growth. We are passionate about uncovering the deeper dimensions of sonship, with a passion for the Hebrew language.

As a Christ-centred mystic, I serve a pastoral role, podcaster, and ascension coach, guiding our community through transformative journeys unpacking new creation living. With a BA degree in Theology, I additionally facilitate these spiritual explorations through writing books and presenting courses at Throne Room Mystic Academy. Subscribe to my Patreon page for additional ascensions and teachings to empower your sonship.

info@throneroommystic.com

www.throneroommystic.com

Subscribe to my Patreon page:

patreon.com/ThroneRoomMystic

FaceBook:	@throneroommystic
	@Centre stage Christian Church
	@WellsofMem
	@Scharl van Staden
YouTube:	@Throneroommystic
	@TheWellsofMem

Heaven's Heart for Earth

Seraph Creative is a collective of artists, writers, theologians & illustrators who desire to see the body of Christ grow into full maturity, walking in their inheritance as Sons of God on the Earth.

Sign up to our newsletter to know about future exciting releases.

Visit our website: www.seraphcreative.org

www.ingramcontent.com/pod-product-compliance
Lightning Source LLC
Chambersburg PA
CBHW071324120626
46546CB00002B/435